Leatherneck Sea Stories

Leatherneck Sea Stories

Recollections of Marines, Korea, and the Corps of the 1950s

Dave Easton

CANOPIC
PUBLISHING

Gatlinburg, Tennessee

Canopic Publishing
1843 Hidden Hills Rd
Gatlinburg, TN 37738
www.canopicpublishing.com

Book design by Phil Rice
Cover design by Gheorghe Stratan and Jonathan Williams
Conceptual consultation by Alan Phillips

Library of Congress Cataloging-in-Publication Data

Easton, Dave, 1932-
Leatherneck sea stories : recollections of Marines, Korea, and the Corps of
the 1950s / by Dave Easton. — 1st ed.
p. cm.
ISBN 978-0-9728604-5-1 (alk. paper)
1. Easton, Dave, 1932- 2. United States. Marine Corps—Military life. 3.
United States. Marine Corps—Biography. 4. Korean War, 1950-1953—
Personal narratives, American. I. Title.

VE23.E37 2007
359.9'6092—dc22
[B]

2007032709

Printed in the United States of America
10 9 8 7 6 5 4 3 2 1
First Edition

Dedicated to
those Marines known
as
"The Chosin Few."

They deserve much more.

Table of Contents

Preface

With the exception of the article titled "Red," all the events and characters described in the following pages took place between January 1951 and December 1953 during my first hitch in the Corps. "Red" begins in February of 1957 at Quantico, and goes to mid-1958 when Red was sent to Okinawa. There was a brief reunion in 1962 worth mentioning but that was at the tail end of my second hitch, which with a two-year extension lasted five years. There were many memorable Marines and events from the second enlistment that should justly be a part of this book but by the time readers reach the end of this compilation they will be ready for a break. My health and memory permitting, another volume might be considered for the future—but I don't want to get too far ahead of myself.

While some of the content may have historical significance, this book is not intended to be a history of the Corps or the Korean conflict. I'll leave that effort to others more inclined for such endeavors. As the title suggests, this is a gathering of memories from one Marine's experiences. I apologize for the occasional redundancy between stories but they were written individually with no thought of ever being combined into chronological order. Similarly, the "Glossary of Marine Speak" is an informal listing of terms relevant to the writing but in no way represents a complete or scholarly treatment of the language of Marines (besides, some of the language of Marines might best be left out of print!). The photos and other illustrations are from my personal collection and, while not exactly fine works of art, are sentimental mementoes that hopefully complement the stories. If I have failed to acknowledge the photographer of the snapshots, please forgive the omission but such are the details that get lost over time.

Simply stated, this is a book about Marines. I hope that the text that follows conveys a sense of the men described, the times as they were then, and a small bit of the pleasure and pride that I have retained over the last half century from having been blessed with such comrades-in-arms.

Leatherneck Sea Stories

Glossary of
Marine Speak

Terms a reader may encounter in the reading of these chronicles:

A as in Able

Airburst: An artillery shell or aerial bomb fused so as to explode prior to impact with the ground.

Airdale: Member of an aviation unit. Also used to refer to members of the Air Force, sometimes called Fly Boys or Zoomies.

Amtrak: An armored amphibious tractor used in amphibious landings, usually to put the first and second waves of assault troops on the beach. Subsequent waves would come ashore in landing craft of various sizes depending on cargo.

AP: Short for Armor Piercing. A type of ammunition usually employed against enemy armor or fortified positions. The explosive charge in the nose was designed to provide maximum penetration prior to detonation.

B as in Baker

BAM: An acronym for "Broad-Assed Marine," an unflattering term used to refer to the early women Marines.

Battalion: A Marine unit consisting of three rifle and one weapons companies. It is the base self-sustaining unit in the Corps and numbers approximately 1200 men.

BAR: Abbreviation for Browning Automatic Rifle. This weapon fired fully automatic at two cyclic rates of fire, and in the hands of a trained shooter was capable of single-shot fire as well. It was fed from 20-round magazines. There were nine BARs in a rifle platoon and twenty-seven in a Marine rifle company.

Bazooka: A shoulder-fired rocket launcher. Early models in Korea were leftover from WWII and proved inadequate for stopping more modern armor. The replacement weapons were of larger bore and did the trick.

Below: Aboard ship this referred to any deck below the main deck. In a building it was anything at a lower level than your current position.

Birdlegs: A nickname often assigned to a Marine who has no muscle definition in the calf area of his legs. There was a squad leader in our company with legs like pencils and he was never referred to by name. He was either "Birdlegs" or "Sgt. Birdlegs," depending on who was speaking to or about him.

Boondocks: Anyplace in the field whether on maneuvers or in a combat theater. Once you left civilized areas you were in the boondocks.

Boondockers: Field shoes issued prior to around 1952 when they were replaced by 10-inch boots. Boondockers were worn with lace-up canvas leggings that came to just below the knee.

Boot: A term ascribed to a recruit in the Marine Corps or the Navy. The basic training for these two services is known as boot camp. The term boot is also used to refer to someone with less time in service than the person using the term.

Brig: In civilian life it is called a jail or prison. In the Army it is the stockade. In the Marines and Navy it is called the brig. The brigs I saw aboard ship were usually situated in close proximity to the engine room so they were both noisy and hot.

Brig Rat: A person who has served a long or perhaps

multiple sentences in the brig. There was a time when a rated Marine could not be confined, so a stripe or two on the arm gave one a measure of security. A reduction in grade and loss of pay and privileges kept a lot of guys out of the brig.

Bulkhead: A wall or any partition separating one area from another.

C as in Charlie

Cannon Cocker: Anyone assigned to an artillery unit. Artillery guys will tell you that artillery is what brings dignity to what would otherwise just be a brawl.

Carbine: A small shoulder fired weapon. Usually the personal weapon of lieutenants, staff NCOs, and some members of crew served weapon sections. A magazine fed piece capable of fully automatic fire. Was not favorably thought of as it tended to jam and was unreliable in cold weather.

Chicken or Kid: Either of these two terms were applied to a very young or youthful appearing member of a unit. These terms were primarily used by the vets from WWII.

Chiggie Bears: Members of the Korean Service Corps (KSC). These were usually older Koreans who were assigned to Marine units. They carried supplies, dug trenches, laid barbed wire and performed all manner of other physical labors. They were not armed and were always under the supervision of one or more Marines while working. There was a lot of speculation that some of these guys were spies and passing info to the Gooks.

Civvies: Marine speak for civilian clothes.

CP: Abbreviation for Command Post. This would be wherever the unit commander set up shop.

Company: A Marine unit of about 220 men and seven officers. Companies were always identified by a letter. There were three rifle and one weapons company to a battalion.

C-Rations: The main source of sustenance for troops on line. They came in a box consisting of three canned meals and an accessory packet. The accessory packet had toilet paper, cigarettes, toothbrush, etc. The C-Rations we were eating in 1952 were World War II surplus and carried dates in the 40s on the packaging.

D as in Dog

Deck: The ground, the floor, or anything underfoot. When shot at, one "hit the deck." If knocked down, one had been "decked."

Division: A Marine unit composed of three rifle regiments and all supporting arms, approximately 22,000-25,000 troops. The Marine Corps currently has three divisions authorized. During WWII, there were six divisions of Marines.

Doggy: A rather uncomplimentary term used to describe soldiers in the U.S. Army. Other variations could be dogface or doggie. I don't know the origin or the history of this terminology, it is just something that worked its way into Marine-speak.

E as in Easy

Entrenching Tool: There were two models in use. The most frequently issued was a small folding shovel. The other was a small pick mattock. Both fit into a heavy duty canvas carrier that attached to a pack in such a manner as to be accessible at all times. The pick handle was a favorite of some Marines to use as a blackjack when they went out on "snatch teams" to try and bring back a prisoner.

Executive Officer: Every unit company-sized or larger had an XO. He was second in command and acted as the commanding officer's right-hand man.

EE/8: Known throughout the Corps in those days as a "Double Easy 8." It was a telephone in a canvas case that had a crank on the side to ring up whoever controlled the network. If you have ever watched the TV show *M*A*S*H**, you have seen Radar O'Reilly crank a Double Easy 8.

F as in Fox

Fire in the Hole: A warning shouted to alert other Marines that something is about to be blown up.

Fire Team: The smallest unit of maneuver in the Marine Corps. It consists of four Marines built around a BAR. Normally a corporal is fire team leader. There is a rifleman scout, another rifleman who acts as assistant BAR man and carries extra magazines, and the BAR man. There are three fire teams to a squad that is under the direction of a sergeant. In today's Marine Corps, the BAR is passé and has been replaced by what is referred to as a SAW or Squad Automatic Weapon. The SAW fires a smaller round and is belt fed, which is a definite improvement in firepower, but old time Marines will always have a soft spot for the BAR.

G as in George

Gooks or Goonies: Names attached to the North Koreans and Chinese by the Marines.

Gooneyland: Where the Gooks and Goonies lived. The other side of no-man's land, which was between their barbed wire and ours.

Grab ass: There were two types. The first was horseplay by one or more guys, wrestling and such or fooling around in formation. They were often ordered to "Knock off the grab ass!" The other was called organized grab ass. Time off was given for organized grab ass and a variety of events was sponsored. One had a choice but everyone had to participate in some event.

Green Side Out: The reference here is to the helmet cover once worn exclusively by Marines. It has a camouflage pattern on both sides, one side being green, the other brown. It was common when there was the least sign of confusion in the ranks for some wag to shout "green side out" or "brown side out" depending on which was the opposite of the side then showing.

Grunt: Description of a Marine infantryman. This term actually came more into favor I think during the Vietnam conflict. Another term applied to the jarheads in the trenches was "Snuffy."

H as in How
Hatch: Any doorway or passageway between areas.
Head: Bathroom.
Head Call: A trip to the bathroom. A "head detail" would be an assignment to clean the bathroom.
HE: Stands for high explosive. Another kind of ammunition, usually fired at enemy troops and positions to inflict casualties and destroy fortifications.
Hitch: Term of enlistment. For example, a 3-year hitch. It can also apply to how many enlistments a person had. For example, a person who had reenlisted twice after his first hitch would be on his third hitch.
HMG: Short for heavy machine gun. The difference between an LMG (light machine gun) and a heavy was that a LMG was air cooled and an HMG was water cooled.
Hootch: Also called Hootchie. This was what Marines called the bunkers in which they lived and in some cases from which they fought.

I as in Item

J as in Jig

K as in King

L as in Love
Ladder: Stairwells or ladders.
Leatherneck: A synonym for Marine dating back to the days of sailing ships when cutlasses and swords were the weapons with which most battles were fought. The Marines wore a high protective collar made of thick leather, hence the term "leatherneck." The collar of the Marine dress blue uniform of today has a collar that pays homage to the tradition of the leatherneck of the past.
LMG: light machine gun. The difference between Light

and Heavy guns is explained under HMG.

Luke: Another nickname for the enemy, short for "Luke the Gook."

M as in Mike

M1: Standard issue rifle to Marines in the 1950 era. Fired semi-automatic and was clip fed with 8 rounds at a time. Weighed about 9.5 pounds and had an effective range of 500 yards in the hands of a trained marksman.

MLR: Abbreviation for main line of resistance.

Mortars: A weapon with a high angle of fire that can reach defilade areas protected from direct fires. There were several sizes of mortars available to the Marines in Korea. At the company level there were three 60mm tubes. At the battalion level there were bigger mortars with more range that were 81mm in bore. At the regimental level there were 4.2 inch mortars available for support.

MOS: Short for military occupational specialty. Each field of endeavor was identified by a four-digit number. For instance, a basic infantryman fell into the 0300 field. A trained rifleman became 0311, a machine gunner in a rifle company was 0331, and a mortar man was 0341.

N as in Nan

O as in Oboe

OP: Used as another name for an outpost. These were positions in front of the MLR that served as early warning of approaching enemy forces. In general they were very dangerous places to be.

Organized Grab Ass: See "Grab Ass."

P as in Peter

Pinkies: Office personnel at any unit level. These were the clerk typist types

Piss & Punk: Refers to bread & water. There was a day when Marines and sailors who violated "Rocks & Shoals," which was the military law before the initiation of the Uniform Code of Military Justice (UCMJ), could be sentenced to thirty days confinement on bread and water. Every third day the prisoner was given a full ration. As I recall this sentence was still available to commanding officers aboard ship but not in the States as recently as the mid-50s.

Piss Tube: A used 155mm artillery shell, open at both ends, one of which is buried in the ground. The inside of the tube and the ground around it were sprinkled with lime and the result was a urinal for all hands. The term "piss tube" was also sometimes used by riflemen to disparagingly refer to mortars, regardless of bore size.

Platoon: A Marine unit made up of three squads of thirteen men each, a platoon guide, a platoon sergeant, and commanded by a second lieutenant. After the squad, this was the closest knit group in the Corps.

Pogey Bait: Used to describe sweets. Candy, ice cream, and cookies would all be classified as "pogey bait."

Pogue: This would be a rear echelon trooper. A clerk in a PX would be a pogue to an artilleryman. An artilleryman, on the other hand, would be a pogue to a rifleman. Actually, everyone is a pogue compared to a rifleman. However, in defense of pogues, they are still Marines and every Marine is a rifleman and I have seen cooks, bakers, and pinkies all put into the line when necessary and they conducted themselves admirably.

Police Call: When "police call" was sounded all hands had to turn to and clean up the unit area. This meant picking up all visible trash. On some bases there was a billet for a "Police Sgt." His responsibilities had nothing whatsoever to do with catching bad guys. He was the one who made sure that grass got cut, hedges trimmed, etc.

Poncho: A square sheet of rubberized fabric with a hole in the center and a row of snaps down two opposite sides of the square. One could put his head through the hole, snap the sides, and stay relatively dry from the knees up.

Poop: News! If someone thought you knew something they

didn't, you would be asked, "What's the poop?" The word scoop was also used in a very similar manner and more frequently.

PRC-6: More commonly referred to by civilians as a walkie-talkie. Marines called them Prick-6s. They had a reputation for being very unreliable and the worse you needed them, the more unreliable they seemed to be. Among other things, on long patrols in cold weather there was a potential for the battery to fail.

Q as in Queen

R as in Roger

Rat Race: At the base in Quantico, Virginia just outside of D.C., the government sponsored a Saturday evening dance at the enlisted men's club. Busloads of women were trucked in from the capital for this weekly event. To the Marines of the base it was known as the Rat Race.

Regiment: A Marine unit consisting of three battalions and supporting arms. Regiments are identified by a number followed by the word Marines. For example, I served in the 6th Regiment (6th Marines) and the 5th Regiment (5th Marines). There are three infantry regiments to a division.

Re-Up: To reenlist for another hitch. There was a reenlistment bonus associated with reenlisting. I don't recall exactly, but a 6-year reenlistment carried a bonus of about $2,000. Wow!

Roger: On a radio, this term was used to acknowledge that a message had been received and was understood.

S as in Sugar

Salt: A Marine who had lengthy service was classified as a salt or as an old salt. The derivation of the term comes from the time spent aboard ship on the ocean and was evidenced by the color of one's dungarees which had become very light in color through repeated salt water washings. Next to rank, time in the Corps was the second criteria for deciding who got the shit details and who didn't.

Scoop: The latest scoop could be insignificant gossip or the night's patrol route. Having been told the latest scoop, a Marine could be considered to have gotten the word!

Scuttlebutt: This term has a dual purpose. First it is the name given to a drinking fountain. It also is used to describe rumor or unsubstantiated information. In other words, "scuttlebutt has it that . . ."

Sea Stories: When a group of Marines get together to exchange ideas and tales about subjects of any nature—ranging from the girls back home, yesterday's battle, or world politics—the subject matter, the speaker and the truth or fiction of the statements are irrelevant. The conversations are considered as "telling sea stories."

Seven-Eighty-Two Gear: Everything a jarhead needed to survive in the boondocks. Cartridge belt, canteens & mess gear, tent with poles and pegs, etc. No idea why it was called thus.

Shelter Half: One half of a tent, one pole and five pegs. In order to construct a tent a Marine had to buddy up with a fire team member to get the other half of the tent, the missing pole and the number of stakes requisite to secure the tent in a stable manner.

Shitbirds: A species who never seemed to get the job done in a military manner. Some were washed out in boot camp but some made it through and depending on their MOS and the sergeant to which assigned could live a miserable existence.

Short Round: Usually a friendly northbound mortar or artillery round passing overhead that for one reason or another comes down too soon and lands closer to friendly troops than to the enemy. "Short round" was also a term applied to Marines of short stature and was interchangeable with "skosh."

Sister Services: Army, Navy, Air Force, and Coast Guard.

Six and a Kick: Description of a sentence for a serious

violation of military law. The translation is six months of confinement and a bad conduct discharge. Only a DD (dishonorable discharge) was more serious.

Skipper: A term applied to refer to the commanding officer, usually at the company level.

Skoshi/Skosh: The Korean word "skoshi" means small, little, not a lot. So anyone who was not tall was immediately nicknamed "Skosh." It was used quite frequently to denote a shortage or insufficiency of food, water, or ammo.

Slop Chute: It didn't matter which base you were stationed at, the designation for the Enlisted Men's Club was slop chute. As time went by these institutions became more segregated by rank. The NCOs had their own clubs and the snuffys had theirs.

Snapping In: In the truest sense, to snap in is to practice developing the correct aiming procedure for firing weapons. In general use the term applies to anything one is learning or trying to perfect.

Snoop & Poop: Refers to the practice of doing work in the boondocks, usually on one's stomach in the weeds or bushes. To practice squad or fire team tactics in the field would be a classic example of snooping and pooping.

Snuffy: The same as the modern day grunt

Sound Power: This was a communication system widely employed in Korea. It required wires to be run between phones. The entire area of Korea in the vicinity of where the hostilities took place was under about a foot of the wire when the truce was signed.

Squad: A Marine unit of thirteen men. Three four-man fire teams led by a buck sergeant. Three squads formed the basis for a platoon.

Stand-By: Whenever a delay occurred the troops were told to stand by, usually for the latest scoop. Stand by also represented a state of readiness. When you were on stand by it was probable that you would ship out or be moved forward on very short notice. Of course, the outfit jokers had a lot of fun with the term. For instance, it was common to hear in the ranks "Stand by to stand by. There will be a will be. Fall out in dress blues, tennis shoes, and a light coat of oil."

Swabbie: A member of the Navy. Even corpsmen assigned to the Marines were called swabbies, but in the case of corpsmen, it was done with affection and humor. I'm not sure how widely the term is still in use. I have seen other more recent things where they are referred to as "squids" or "anchor clankers."

T as in Tear

Ten Percent: These were the losers in an outfit. There always seemed to be ten percent who didn't get the word, and if they did, they didn't understand it.

The Word: Orders and instructions coming down through the chain of command. A squad leader or platoon commander briefing his unit might say something like, "OK, listen up! Here's the word!"

Topside: The opposite of below. If you were going from a lower deck to a higher deck, you were going topside.

Toxsan: A Korean word meaning huge or many. We always felt there were toxsan Chinamen not too far away.

Tracer: A type of ammunition which left a phosphorescent trail in its trajectory to the target. In a belt fed weapon like a machine gun every fourth or fifth round was a tracer and allowed the gunner to adjust his aim point without seeing the impact zone.

Troop and Stomp: In garrison it was not unusual to have one or more hours a day of close order drill. This consisted of marching and the manual of arms. To the troops this was known as "troop and stomp."

U as in Uncle

V as in Victor

W as in Willie

WP, or Willie Peter: This was the abbreviation for white phosphorus ammunition that could be fired by mortar or artillery. When it burst there were dense clouds of thick white smoke and could be used to mark targets or to screen movement. In addition, it was a fearsome weapon to exposed troops because white phosphorous was capable of burning through metal and was very difficult to extinguish. Willie Peter was also made available in hand grenade form.

X as in X-Ray
XO: Short form for executive officer.

Y as in Yoke

Z as in Zebra

Bob Fargo and me sporting our new haircuts

The Beginning

When World War II ended I was still in high school, and with the war raging in Europe and Asia during my formative years, there was no avoiding growing up in a wartime culture. In many ways I think this had a long-term effect on my attitudes and many years later made it extremely difficult for me to understand what I perceived to be a lack of patriotism in the younger generations. During my teen years the country had been solidly behind what everyone I knew considered to be the righteousness of our cause, and patriotism was at an all time high. Hitler was considered a plague. The Japanese were as bad, or in my mind, worse because of their sneak attack at Pearl Harbor and their subsequent barbarism toward American prisoners.

Perhaps because by the time I had matured enough to take an interest and have a grasp of the conflict, the Germans were on the run, I became more interested in the campaign in the Pacific, which was primarily a Marine Corps operation. Also, my older brother was serving with the Navy in the Pacific theatre. The end result of this interest was that I developed a profound respect and admiration for the Marines, both as a fighting force and for the individuals who were so dedicated to their country and their Corps. I didn't know it then but a few years later I would be privileged to meet and serve with some of these Marines. Today, more than half a century later, I still revere and honor the memories of those men who were heroes to me.

Having finished high school in 1949, I was working at a small print shop at the intersection of Lake Street and North Michigan Avenue in Chicago. The ride on the train to my home on the South Side each evening was about forty minutes. Normally I passed this time reading the afternoon paper, which back then was *The Herald Examiner*. From mid-1950 on, the chief news items were related to the invasion of South Korea by its northern neighbor. As the situation deteriorated and American troops were committed to the fighting, the items became more disturbing. The stories of the outright assassination of American GIs, with their hands bound behind their backs with barbed wire, was reminiscent of the way in which the Japanese had treated prisoners during World War II.

In mid-1950 the Marines arrived in Korea, and after a brilliant amphibious landing at Inchon in September, were ordered to march north. After having driven the North Koreans to the northernmost extremities of the peninsula, the 1st Marine Division was surrounded near the Yalu River by a vastly numerically superior force of Chinese "volunteers" who had infiltrated into the mountains that encircled the Chosin Reservoir. There was much doom and gloom in the news about the expected loss of the entire division caught in the trap. As it turned out, the Marines marched over 70 miles to the sea, not only extricating themselves from the trap, but inflicting heavy casualties on the surrounding force in the process. Many of the officers and non-coms who led these Marines were Pacific campaign veterans who had been activated from the reserve. Once again, my heroes had performed a military miracle. Again I was privileged to later meet and serve with many of the men who survived the "March to the Sea." The survivors of this campaign became known as "The Chosin Few."

Shortly after the withdrawal from the reservoir at Chosin, a friend of mine from school and sports activities called me to say he was enlisting in the Marines. I don't know why the thought had not yet occurred to me. Before the conversation went much farther I had arranged to go with him to the recruiting office. The only proviso was that I would not leave before my mother's birthday, which was coming up.

Early in January 1951, we presented ourselves in the tower of the old main post office in downtown Chicago for testing and physical examinations. We sailed through with no trouble, although I suspect that because of the situation in Korea, the standards may have been somewhat relaxed. Once accepted, our departure date was established as 21 January. We would be departing Chicago by train and our destination was to be the fabled Marine Recruit Training Center at Parris Island, South Carolina.

Between the time of my enlistment and departure I was both surprised and mildly confused by the actions and behavior of my friends in the neighborhood. At this time the Selective Service Act, better known as the draft, was still in force. All able-bodied males in my age group were registered and if selected would be taken into the Army for two years. My Marine Corps enlistment was for a three-year period, but the Corps at that time was entirely a volunteer outfit. The Army had been and was still taking a bad licking in Korea, and most of my buddies enlisted in the Air Force or the Navy. These were four year enlistments and all I could think of was that they were adding two years to their enlistments to avoid serving as ground troops. This is what confused me because I had never seen any of these guys shy away from a scrap and I was surprised that they wouldn't relish a chance to kick some Chinese or North Korean ass.

One other thing that transpired during this time stands out in my memory. One of the guys from the neighborhood who had dropped out of school and joined the Marines rather than go to reform school came home on convalescent leave. He had made the landing at Inchon and had fought and been wounded in the breakout from the Chosin Reservoir. The change in Tom was remarkable. When I had known him earlier he was beyond the juvenile delinquent stage and was a prime candidate for prison. He now had a courteous manner and exuded confidence and pride. If the Marines could work a change like that on a tough kid like Tom, I knew I had picked the right outfit. (I have since learned that Tom has gone on to his next duty station. God speed & Semper Fi Tom.)

As instructed, Bob and I arrived at Union Station on the 21st. We reported to a booth manned by a couple of sergeants dressed in what we would come to know as "undress blues," khaki shirts over blue trousers with the red stripes authorized only for non-commissioned officers as a memorial of the Battle of Chapultapec. They checked us in against a list of scheduled departees and issued us meal tickets to use in the dining car in route. The train ride was uneventful except for meeting some of the other hopeful Marines-to-be. Along the route the train added cars with enlistees from Michigan and Ohio. When we arrived in Washington, D.C., a major switching took place and cars carrying guys from New England, New York, and Pennsylvania were added. The train then turned south and we headed for Parris Island. All of us had heard stories of what awaited us there but none of us believed it would be as bad as we had been told.   HAH!

I cannot recall exactly where it was we detrained and boarded buses, but I think it was in a place called Yemmasee. I know we traveled through towns named Rocky Mount and Port Royal. The difference in the countryside from what I was used to in Chicago was interesting. I remember standing on the platform between train cars as it passed over mile after mile of trestles built five or six feet above the first real swamp I had ever seen.

Once the transfer to buses was complete, we were on the final leg of the trip. The January temperature was hovering just barely above the freezing mark and a nasty little drizzle hung in the air. The hour was close to midnight when the buses pulled up in front of the reception center.

We got our first introduction to what our life was to be like when the bus stopped. The doors had barely opened when a very small corporal with a very large voice burst into the aisle and shouted, "Put out those cigarettes and get your lazy asses off this bus and form three ranks on the white lines!! MOVE! MOVE! MOVE!" One of the recruits thought to take a final drag before putting out his cigarette. With no hesitation the corporal smacked the butt out of the recruit's mouth and asked in a roar, "BOY, do you want to eat that cigarette?!" That set the tone and everyone moved smartly off the bus.

After allowing us to stand long enough for the drizzle to soak our civilian clothes and the chill to soak into our bones, our drill instructor appeared. We were advised that life as we had known it was over, AS OF NOW! It was OK with the DI if we wanted to give our souls to Jesus, but we had better never forget that our asses belonged to him. It was shortly after this stirring little speech that I heard for the first time the term "maggot" used in reference to a human being. Of course my frame of reference as to what constituted a human being varied greatly from the opinion held by the drill instructor. I never discussed these differences in perspective with him.

II

We left the receiving area in the closest semblance to a military formation that the DI's could construct with the raw materials available. Our head DI and his two Corporal assistants ranged up and down the ranks berating everyone about everything. It was hard to imagine that a group this size could do so many things wrong in such a short time. The terms "maggot," "shitbird," and "idiot" were interchangeable and applied to all hands.

We were marched single file past the opening of a large tent. As each person drew opposite the opening he was hit in the chest with a blanket, a mattress cover, two sheets and a pillowcase. At the next tent, we entered one end carrying the blanket, mattress cover, sheets, pillowcase, and whatever civilian luggage we had brought with us. We emerged at the other end carrying all the above plus a 4-

inch thick mattress to fit a folding cot and a pillow.

Once reformed into three ranks, we were marched a considerable distance and halted on the so-called company street between the two facing rows of tents which housed our platoon. Anywhere else the street would have been called a boardwalk, but if the DI said it was a street, by God, I'll have to fight the first man who says otherwise. The tents had a wooden floor (deck), a pot bellied stove in the center, and six cots around the perimeter. We were split into 6-man groups, assigned to tents, and told to make up our bunks and go to sleep. It was well past 2 a.m. and still drizzling when we finally turned in. Reveille sounded at 4 a.m. that morning and every morning thereafter for the next eight weeks. From one perspective we may have been fortunate. Boot camp was normally twelve weeks, but because of the manpower demands of Korea, the program had been shortened to 8 weeks. I'm convinced that what it lacked in duration was made up for in intensity.

My friend Bob, who I enlisted with, was one of my tent mates. In fact, we would remain together in the same unit for about a year and a half. We were finally split up when I left for Korea on an earlier replacement draft than him. The other guys in our tent were a very diverse group. Billy Poole had left college to enlist in the Corps. He was from Mississippi, and where else would he have gone to school except "Ole Miss," where he had been a running back on the football team. Billy was a little older than the rest of us and upon reflection I would also say that by virtue of his football training he was in better physical condition, too. Upon graduation from boot camp, Billy was assigned to a fairly new weapons detachment at Camp LeJeune. These were the 4.5" Rockets fired in "ripples" of 144 at a time from a truck or helicopter transported launcher. I never saw Billy again after the completion of boot training but I did hear he had attained the rank of staff sergeant when I was still a PFC.

Bob Fargo was another tent mate. Bob was the tallest member of our platoon and contrary to the practice of assigning the shortest recruit to be the platoon guidon bearer, our DI's went the opposite way and Bob was our platoon guide. After boot, Bob was assigned as a guard at one of the Naval prisons.

Dave Grana was the fifth man in the tent. He was a big strong kid and the youngest among us, but he looked and acted older than his years. He was the rebel in the tent who would try to sneak smokes and dodge details. After being caught and chastised a few times he began to observe the rules. Dave was assigned to a motor transport battalion upon completion of boot and I did see him a couple of times in Korea when his unit hauled our sorry asses hither, thither, and yon. After discharge from the service Dave married his childhood sweetheart and they opened a bar. It was more of a roadhouse actually. It was located outside any incorporated area and as a result drew a lot of late night business after the city bars closed. On at least two separate occasions Dave had disputes with rowdy customers that ended in shots being fired and in both cases the customers lost. Makes me wonder why Dave hadn't been an infantry type.

Armand Briere, better known as Blackie, was the final member of our tent crew. Blackie, Bob Garza, and I all ended up with orders to the 6th Marines, where Blackie and I became two of the three BAR Men in the same squad. Blackie hailed from a resort town in upstate New York and worked as a lifeguard, waiter, and whatever else at Lake George. His outdoor activities and exposure to the sun are what earned him the nickname. French was the spoken language in his home and he was fluent, which came in handy when we were in North Africa. Blackie took advantage of an offer to transfer to the 8th Marines and go on a second Med cruise in mid 1952, thereby missing out on an opportunity to get to Korea.

During that first night I was both very tired and very cold, so I removed only my shoes. This made it a bit easier at 4 a.m. to respond quickly to the fever pitch insisted upon by the DI's. Once again we were formed into three ranks in the company street. The wooden street had glazed over slightly during the night and there were more than a few spills as the recruits attempted to comply with the shouted orders to "MOVE! MOVE! MOVE!" As the good sergeant said, all he wanted to see were "assholes and elbows. MOVE!"

The first order of business was for the drill instructors to establish a few rules. Smoking was permissible only if the DI informed the platoon that "the smoking lamp is lit," and all smoking was to be done only in formation. Not being a smoker at the time, the restriction on smoking had no effect on me. However, several times a day a formation was called expressly to allow guys to smoke, and even though you might be a non-smoker, you still had to make the formations.

At reveille we would form ranks immediately for physical training, called calisthenics in civilian life. We would then be given time to make up our bunks in the prescribed manner. A very definitely prescribed manner it was too, I might add. At the next formation we would be marched as a group to the head where we would have an allotted time to perform our "S's," those being shit, shower, shave, and shampoo, all but the first being mandatory. Later, after we had been issued dress shoes, we acquired another S. That would be shine, also mandatory.

After a return to the tent to stow our shaving gear, we reformed and were marched about a mile to the mess hall for breakfast. We made this round trip three times a day, but it was much more than just going to eat. During the trip, in both directions, the drill instructors swarmed around and through the formation, offering unsolicited but emphatic criticisms and comments on our posture, marching abilities, intelligence, and heritage. Personally, I was able to avoid a lot of individual attention as a result of knowing close order drill and facing movements from two years of ROTC in high school. There were days, however, when the DI's decided to use peer pressure and resorted to group punishment where we all suffered together.

One thing every Marine will recall is the cadence counted by his drill instructor. Each one had his own way of sounding off, and most Marines if and when they became NCOs and had to march troops, fell back on this to develop their own cadence call. In addition to counting cadence, our DI insisted that we lean back and dig our heels into the ground as we marched, sometimes substituting the words "HEELS, HEELS, HEELS" for the cadence. By the end of boot camp the heels on our boondockers were ready for the cobbler's shop. Frequently we were given the command to "count cadence count!" At this point the platoon would sound off in unison "ONE TWO THREE FOUR, ONE TWO THREE FOUR." The odd numbers sounded as the left heel struck the ground and the even numbers as the right heel hit the ground. When our DI in his infinite wisdom felt we had earned the privilege to speak about his Marine Corps, we were allowed to chant "ONE TWO THREE FOUR, WE LOVE THE MARINE CORPS."

As we marched from place to place on the post, it was common to pass other platoons in various stages of training. At the beginning we did not compare well at all with platoons that were in their later weeks. While these differences were obvious to us, they were further pointed out and elaborated upon by our DI's. It was a very good feeling in later weeks to pass a newly arrived platoon. They would be struggling to keep in step and maintain alignment and we would go past them, our heels all hitting the ground in unison, sounding like one man marching. Probably more like one man with very big feet marching.

III

One of the challenges associated with our three daily trips to the mess hall was to avoid being designated as a "shitbird." It was a rare trip indeed when this dubious distinction was not awarded to one or another of our number. Often the nominee was ignorant of the reason for his selection, but once designated there was no appeal. The drill went something like this:

Drill Instructor: "Platoon HALT"

(He would then approach the targeted recruit and place his face about one inch from the recruit's nose.)

Drill Instructor: "Doe are you a shitbird?"

Recruit: "Sir, no sir!"

Note: Whenever addressing a DI it was mandatory to open and close all commentary with the word "sir." Or as our DI put it to us on our first night at Parris Island, "When you speak to me or any other Marine the first and last words out of your filthy mouths had better be 'sir' or you'll eat those words."

Drill Instructor: "Well, I think you *are* a shitbird! Are you calling me a liar?"

Recruit: "Sir, no sir!"

Drill Instructor: "No sir what, shitbird? You're not a shitbird or you're not calling me a liar?"

Recruit: "Sir, no sir. I was not calling you a liar."

Drill Instructor: "Ah hah! So if I'm not a liar I was right, you are a shitbird, aren't you?"

Recruit: "Sir, yes sir!"

Drill Instructor: "O.K. shitbird, let me see you fly!"

Recruit: "Sir, I cannot fly sir."

Drill Instructor: "JESUS CHRIST! I knew you didn't have the makings of a Marine in your sorry ass. Now I find out you aren't even acceptable shitbird material!"

Here the DI gives the commands necessary to restart the platoon in the direction of the mess hall. The mess hall had two single door entries about six feet apart. When the platoon arrived we were broken into two parallel files, one to enter each door. All other platoons eating here exercise the same procedure. At this point the shitbird of the day is called forth and placed between the two entry doors with his back to the mess hall, facing the oncoming files. As the files move past he is to raise and lower his arms in imitation of flight while repeating over and over in a loud voice:

"I'm a shitbird, but I cannot fly!"

When all the troops were inside he was allowed to fall in at the end of the chow line. To the drill instructors' credit they never went through the line until all their recruits had been served.

There was another little game the DI's played after we had been issued rifles. Only recruits who were foolish enough to refer to their rifle as a gun were eligible for these festivities. The offender and his rifle were placed in a place of prominence where there was sure to be a high volume of passers by. His instructions were as follows and to be repeated until the DI told him to stop:

> *Right Hand brandishing rifle and shouting:*
> "This is my rifle."
> *Left Hand grabbing crotch and shouting:*
> "This is my gun."
> *Right Hand brandishing rifle and shouting:*
> "This is for fighting."
> *Left Hand grabbing crotch and shouting:*
> "This is for fun."

Moving right along, it has often been emphasized that "Every Marine is a rifleman." To try to illustrate the emphasis placed on this, consider that boot camp was eight weeks in duration and two weeks or 25% of that time was spent in marksmanship training. At the time we could not appreciate the connection between some of the training and pulling a trigger. After all, that's all it takes to fire a rifle!

The first week on the rifle range was spent performing exercises referred to as snapping in or dry firing. The intent was to educate each Marine what it was he was supposed to see before he squeezed the trigger. This was called a "sight picture." A correct sight picture was the relationship between the rear and front sight of the rifle and the positioning of that relationship relative to the target being aimed at. At the same time we were being educated on aligning sights we were also being taught how to adjust the rifle sling to minimize movement of the piece during recoil. The sling adjustments were different for each of the four positions we would be expected to fire from on qualification day. These positions were offhand (standing), kneeling, sitting, and prone. We came to believe however that both the sling adjustments and the firing positions were part of a carefully derived plan to allow the DI's to further disburse discomfort without resorting to flagrant violence.

The worst position for me personally was sitting. It all began with sitting with legs crossed at the ankles in front of you facing at a 45 degree angle from the target. The sling was then wrapped around your left arm as tight as necessary to keep your left elbow centered below the rifle. Then both elbows were placed inside the knees and you were expected to lean forward to lay your cheek against the stock to develop the revered sight picture. What I hated about this was that the DI never believed you were far enough forward and would come up behind you and literally sit on your shoulders. We would spend hours each day snapping in at targets reduced in size to simulate those we would fire at over longer ranges when we actually started shooting. These targets were mounted on posts approximately 25 yards distant. There were three targets to each post: one near the top to practice the offhand position, another about two thirds of the way down for use in sighting from the sitting and kneeling positions and the last one just above ground level for prone position practice.

At the conclusion of the snapping in period, we moved to the rifle range. When we were not actually firing, we worked in the pits marking targets for the shooting platoons. These pits were called "the butts." The targets were on tracks that could be raised and lowered. There were two recruits assigned to each target. Targets were "run up" when the commence fire command was given. We would then watch and listen for a bullet to strike the target we were manning. In slow fire, the target was lowered and marked after each hit, and then raised so the shooter could make sight adjustments as required to get into the black. We had two sets of markers, one smaller than the other for use at the 200- and 300-yard ranges, the larger size for use at the 500-yard firings. The markers were reversible, one side

Me, Bob Garza & Don Ragoni

Bob, John "The Greek" Kyritsi, and Baum

*The guy in the foreground is Bob; the cot and
laundry in the background are mine.*

being white and the other black. The targets were also black and white and the color of the marker being hoisted was placed in contrast to the area of the target that had been hit. We had two other pieces of equipment in the butts: A paste pot and patches, again in two colors, for repairing the bullet holes to avoid confusion in marking the next shot. The other was a red flag mounted on a long pole. This was used only when a request to mark a target was given and no strike could be found. The red flag was called "Maggie's Drawers" and it was not something a Marine recruit ever wanted to see. Too many Maggie's Drawers and one could count on going back to the snapping in process at the end of the firing exercise each day.

Eventually we arrived at the day when it was our turn to shoot. We fired every day for a week, with the last day being qualifying day. We each got to fire 50 rounds. A bulls-eye was worth five points and the highest possible score was 250 points. In order to qualify a Marine needed a minimum score of 190. A qualifying shooter was given a Marksman Badge. A score of 210 earned the shooter a Sharpshooter Badge, and 220 was considered Expert and qualified the shooter for the Expert Badge. At one time the Marines who qualified in the top two categories were rewarded with extra pay each month. I don't know if this practice is still in effect but I believe present-day Marine promotion policies factor in an individuals most recent qualification score. The firing sequence began at 200 yards, slow fire ten rounds offhand. This was followed by ten rounds rapid fire sitting position. Since the capacity of the M-1 rifle was only eight rounds, for rapid fire we would load two rounds and a clip. When the commence firing command was given we would fire the two rounds and have to reload a new clip of eight rounds and complete firing within the allotted time before the cease fire command was given. In slow fire the rounds were loaded individually after each shot was taken.

The order was then given to "Pick up your brass and move back to the 300-yard line." At the 300-yard line we would fire ten rounds slow fire, five rounds sitting, and five rounds kneeling. Then using the same loading parameters as at the 200, we would fire ten rounds rapid fire from the prone position. In slow fire the targets were marked after each shot, in rapid fire all ten shots were marked when the "cease fire" order was given. This gave the shooter and the shooting coaches a look at the pattern of the impact area as well as any erratic shots that may have gone astray. After picking up the brass we moved back to the 500-yard marker. Here we fired our final 10 rounds from the prone position, slow fire. Those who did not qualify were given special attention and one more chance a few days later before being set back to do it all again.

All Marines, unless in a combat theater, are required to re-qualify once a year. Later in my career I also qualified with the Browning automatic rifle (BAR), which was my assigned weapon. Even later when I was assigned part-time duty as one of the battalion prison chasers I had to qualify with both the .45 caliber pistol and the 12-guage shotgun. During inspections it was not uncommon for the inspecting officer to ask a Marine, "What is the zero of your rifle at 200 yards?" The officer of course had no way of knowing whether the answer was correct or not, but if it was an infantryman he would know his rifles zero for sure.

By the time we had completed firing for record we began to consider ourselves "old salts." We had become proficient in the manual of arms and close order drill and we had actually begun to fill out the oversize clothes thrown at us that dark, cold night that seemed so long ago. I personally had put on twenty pounds and had never been so fit in my life. We had learned all about military courtesy and the history and tradition of the Marine Corps. However, we still were not Marines in the eyes of our drill instructors and we still had not earned the right to wear the "Eagle, Globe and Anchor."

The final couple of weeks passed rather quickly and the occasions of harassment lessened noticeably as the drill instructors found fewer things to erupt about. The actual graduation ceremony came and went without a hitch. Unlike the politically motivated ceremonies of today, there were no invitations to recruit's families and not a lot of fanfare associated with the event. At the end of the day we all gathered to receive our next duty assignments before going on a 10-day leave. I had requested the infantry and the Corps did not disappoint me. Of course, about 75% of the class received infantry assignments. Most of us were going to the 6th Marine Regiment at Camp Le Jeune. The entire 2nd Division was undergoing a rebuilding after all the warm bodies had been stripped to build the 1st Division to operational readiness for its assignment to Korea.

*Like the DI told us, if you wanna sit, your ass better
fit the bottom of your bucket.*

The Bucket

I don't know about the rest of the Marine Corps, but speaking for the members of recruit platoon #65, we will never see a bucket that doesn't stir a host of memories. Of course it has to look like the buckets we were issued at Parris Island. They were the good old fashioned, galvanized metal type with a sturdy wire handle, and they became a big part of our daily existence and a valued piece of equipment.

Our buckets were given to us as we were herded through the line where we were issued clothes, shoes, towels, and all manner of things. As I recall, the instructions were to place only specific items in the bucket. Since everything we were given was going to the same place, I suspect this was just a ploy to give the DI something to holler about if they found an unauthorized item in a bucket.

Once the issue was complete, we were formed up in ranks. We each had a sea bag on one shoulder and a bucket hanging from the opposite hand as we were marched back to where we were billeted. Buckets were the only authorized seating in our tents, nay, in our existence. Cots were made up immediately upon arising at 4 a.m., and it was forbidden to sit or lie on them again before lights out at 10 p.m. It didn't matter what the size or shape of your hind end was— if you were to sit, your ass better fit the bottom of your bucket.

When we were scheduled for a class or a lecture, the word was always passed to fall out with buckets. The buckets were our seating in class. Given free time to write letters, shine shoes, clean weapons, etc., all of the above were done sitting on the bucket.

Buckets also held sand, and by coincidence, South Carolina seemed to be made up mostly of sand. I suspect it was so to provide a home for the sand fleas that lived there and fed on Marine recruits. In any case, if the platoon or an individual "boot" incurred the wrath of the DI, it frequently resulted in an impromptu exercise session. These sessions involved a bucket of sand being hoisted, lowered, or carried in an assortment of uncomfortable positions for inordinately long periods of time. Of course, at the end of each such session there would be a bucket inspection to satisfy the drill instructors that every single grain of sand had been put back on the surface of South Carolina and that not a single grain remained either inside or was clinging to the outside of any bucket in the platoon. The discovery of a "dirty" bucket would usually result in a repeat of the exercise session, followed by another inspection. This could go on as long as the DI wanted it to.

The bucket also played a role in demonstrations conducted to educate us on the folly of not following orders.

We were given orders to shave every morning. It was totally irrelevant if you had a beard or not, you *would* shave. The drill instructor's philosophy on this was that despite all the odds against it happening, he just might make men and Marines out of a few of us, and we would then need to know how to shave. There were those among us who either didn't take this philosophy to heart or were entirely too casual with the result of their morning effort. If a DI decided that either of the mortal sins described above had been committed, the sinner was sent to his tent with orders to return with his razor and, yep, his bucket—on the double! The platoon was put at "parade rest" while the guilty party was called front and center. There his bucket was placed over his head and with his non-dominant hand he was ordered to take a strain on the handle. He was then ordered to reach up under the bucket and commence shaving. After a stroke or two, the next command given to the shaver was "mark time, double time, march." When their faces healed these guys were faithful shavers for the rest of their time in boot camp.

The bucket also played a role in demonstrating the perils of non-compliance with or disobeying an order. In boot camp it was forbidden to smoke unless the DI gave express permission for each cigarette. He would do so by calling a formation and announcing "The smoking lamp is lit, smoke 'em if you got 'em." Again, there were doubters among us that this was really a rule, and if so, it certainly didn't apply to them. Uh-huh, did too. Being caught smoking without permission also resulted in the violator being sent for his bucket. Instead of his razor he was to bring a full pack of cigarettes. Again, the platoon was put at parade rest, the smoker was called front and center and his bucket was placed over his head. He was then ordered to smoke twenty consecutive cigarettes under the bucket.

What surprises me today is that I have absolutely no recollection of what I did with that bucket when I left Parris Island. I do believe if I could lay my hands on it I might have it bronzed and mounted on a base. The inscription would read something like: "This is my bucket. There are many like it but this one is mine, etc."

Bob Garza, Dick Grant, and Don Estacion

6th Marines

Upon completion of boot camp the entire platoon was authorized a 10-day leave prior to reporting to our next duty stations. Our orders included a delay in transit equivalent to the travel time it would take us to reach our next post plus our 10-day leave allowance. We were also given a travel advance equal to the cost of transportation to reach the new assignment location. Unless your leave destination was between Parris Island and your new assignment, the difference in cost was personal expense. What that meant was that the several of us who were bound for Chicago and Detroit opted for the Greyhound Bus.

While economical, the bus was not the most rapid means of transport. It wound thru places in the Deep South where the depot restaurants and bathrooms were still segregated. For us Northerners, this posed a moral dilemma. Traveling on our bus was a black kid named Weathers who had graduated boot camp with us. He was also a native of Chicago, bound for 29 Palms in California to an artillery regiment assignment. We could do little to protest the segregated restrooms but instead of patronizing the segregated restaurants we bought food at the counters or convenience stores and carried it out to the bus where Weathers was able to join in the culinary delights. Once we got off the bus in Chicago, we never saw Weathers again. In the early '50s the Marine Corps was quasi-segregated. There were "Negroes" in the Corps, but they were, as far as I knew,

49

usually assigned to artillery units as ammo handlers. As I recall, in the combat film footage we were shown of the Pacific island campaigns as part of our "History & Tradition" sessions, there was never a colored Marine in any of the frames. This was not a result of editing the films. At that time blacks were just not assigned to the front line rifle companies.

When our leave time was over and we all had milked the time at home to play future war hero to the fullest extent, we trickled into Camp LeJeune in twos and threes on the appointed day. Personally, I arrived in company with Bob Garza and Dick Grant, at about 10 p.m., just as the lights went out in the barracks. After checking our orders and logging us in, the duty NCO instructed us to find an unoccupied bunk and hit the sack. The sleeping area, known as the "squad bay," was one room that ran the entire length of the barracks. The barracks itself was an H-shaped, 2-story brick building with the offices and heads in the cross-piece of the H. In the squad bay there were steel-framed double-deck bunks along both walls projecting out toward the center of the bay. A double row of wall lockers divided the room and separated the two rows of bunks. I would say that each squad bay accommodated about 100 troops since each barracks housed two companies, one in each wing, and a rifle company was just a little over 200 men. Each company occupied both floors in the wing to which they were assigned.

Once our eyes adjusted to the darkness we could see the unoccupied bunks. Each had a mattress rolled up at the end closest to the wall. Rolled up inside each mattress was a pillow, but there were no sheets or blankets. After traveling from Chicago all day, not having sheets was not a major deal. We all slept well and soundly until reveille at 5:30 a.m. After PT, Police Call and morning chow, all the men who had reported in the evening before were gathered and assigned to platoons, squads, and fire teams. Our new squad leaders then gave us a brief orientation and marched us over to the supply shed where we were issued "782 gear," which in the Corps are the things you need in the field (cartridge belt, packs, mess gear, tent, etc.) Next we were taken to the armory where we were issued weapons. In my case I drew a BAR or, in long form, a Browning Automatic Rifle. When we got back to the barracks we were told not to bother putting anything away but instead to prepare a field transport pack and to put everything else we owned into our sea bag, which was then to be turned in to the supply sergeant. A field transport pack was the largest of the several varieties of packs and included one's blanket rolled into each man's half tent and strapped over the knapsack. It seems that without consulting with any of us the battalion had made arrangements to board ship later that day at Morehead City and to be away from camp for a couple of weeks of amphibious training at Little Creek, Virginia.

Since I will be using letter/number combinations, a word or two of what they symbolize is appropriate. A Marine division consists of three infantry regiments. Regiments are numbered, for example: The 1st Division includes the 1st, 5th, and 7th Regiments. The 2nd Marine Division includes the 2nd, 6th, and 8th Regiments. A number followed by "Marines" identifies a particular regiment, i.e. 6th Marines = 6th Regiment. Each regiment has three rifle battalions always identified by number and always 1st, 2nd, and 3rd. The battalions in turn each have three rifle companies that are always lettered. ABC/1st battalion. DEF/2ndbattalion. GHI/3rd battalion. So, C company, 1st battalion, 6th Marines would be C-1-6 and G company, 3rd battalion 7th Marines would be G-3-7. Simple, huh?

C-1-6—that's Charlie Company, 1st Battalion, 6th Marine Regiment—was truly a unit being reconstituted. That was also true of almost every unit in the Corps, as they had all been drained of warm bodies to bring the 1st Division up to combat strength. The NCOs were almost all reserves who had been recalled, and the senior sergeants and one of the corporals had all seen action in the Pacific against the Japanese. The junior corporals and the senior privates first class who were fire team leaders were also reservists called to active duty, but they were not combat veterans. As time passed the company also received some Korean vets who were either recently discharged from hospitals where they had been recovering from wounds, or they had completed a full tour in Korea and had been rotated back to the States.

These NCOs became my heroes, not just for what they did in the Pacific, but for the way they treated us and for teaching us the survival skills that a Marine infantryman needs to know as well as many lessons about life, in or out of the Corps. As I write this it has been more than 50 years since I have seen any of these men and I still appreciate the role they played in my life and will always feel privileged to have known and served with them.

The time in Little Creek flew by. We first learned all about climbing down cargo nets into landing craft from a tower and then into boats from a ship at sea. What you cannot be taught on the tower is how much you are at the mercy of the sea and what a factor it can be in debarking from a transport into a landing craft. As the ocean swells passed under and around the craft, the ship would rise or fall and the landing craft would do the same, but not always in the same direction. The action of the sea could also cause the distance between the ship and the smaller craft to constantly shift. This would cause the net to become very taut to the extent of almost being pulled out of the landing craft completely. When things moved in the opposite direction the net would go slack and a Marine who had just gone over the rail to descend would find the landing craft coming up to meet him. The worst scenario is when the ship would fall and the landing craft would rise while at the same time the boat and the ship would drift apart. When this occurred the Marines on the sagging net could be suspended between the ship and the net, which eventually at the caprice of the sea would come back together, sometimes with a crash of metal against metal and it was not a good place to be. In such cases the Marines who had already reached the landing craft would hang all their weight on the bottom of the net and try to keep the net from sagging

S/Sgt. Soltner, Sgt. Byrd, Cpl. Black and Sgt. Parks.
Still my heroes, fifty years later.

Lt. Kennington and S/Sgt. Soltner

Over the rail!

*On liberty in Naples in early 1952. Don Estacion, Bob Garza,
The Greek, Wiilie Fromm, Me, Dick Haddad, & Del Edler*

between the two crafts. There were many
who had to be scraped off the sides of th'
but in eight years in the Corps, I only
getting caught in this situation and he was
he only broke an ankle (and I suspect seriou...
skivvies.)

The summer of 1951 went quickly. We spent sev...
days each week in the boondocks. For the majority of the
time we worked on small unit tactics and weapon
employment, usually at the squad and platoon level and
occasionally in company-sized field problems.

The days we weren't in the field we were on
"conditioning hikes." These varied in length and it seemed
the shorter the distance, the faster the pace. They ranged in
distance from five miles to thirty miles and sometimes
included an overnight stay so we could walk home the next
day. Our platoon leader and the other company officers
were true example setters. At some point in the march they
would relieve the men carrying the crew-served weapons.
Having assumed the burden of a machine gun or mortar,
they would then double-time to the front of the formation
to show everyone it wasn't heavy. When not actively
engaged in the activities described above we attended
classes or demonstrations related to our organic weapons
or those that were in support of the infantry. Unless, that is,
we were participating in one form or another of an
inspection.

The one thing that stands out in my mind was that our
training was almost exclusively centered on conducting
offensive operations. This was a reflection of Marine
philosophy. Later when I arrived in Korea this training was
rarely applied in the static trench warfare we encountered.

In September of 1951, the 1st Battalion, 6th Marines
was scheduled to assume the role of the landing party
assigned to the 6th Fleet, which was on station in the
Mediterranean Sea at all times. We left Morehead City, North
Carolina on the 1st of September and lived aboard a Navy
transport ship classified as an APA. The letters had

ething to do with Attack Personnel Assault, and the
p was equipped with davits from which hung about a
ozen LCVPs. Translation: Landing Craft Vehicle Personnel.
During the six months we spent aboard ship, we visited ports
from North Africa to the Greek Isles and many coastal cities
in between. Our home port was Naples, Italy, and we spent
more time there than in any of the other ports. Between
ports-of-call we made amphibious landings on what seemed
to us at the time to be every island, beach, and rock between
Gibraltar and Athens.

During the time between boot camp and returning from
the Med, Bob Garza and I had remained good friends but we
both had begun to form other, different friendships with
mostly the members of our platoon and our company. Bob's
interests when going ashore leaned more to the museum
visit and souvenir purchasing type of outing. As for myself
and the group I had been developing closer associations
with, we seemed to gravitate toward a different type of
experience. Namely, we ended up in the waterfront bistros
and bars where life was much more exciting. The members
of this group, not in order of importance, were John (the
Greek) Kyritsi, Dick (Big Steve) Haddad, Willie (Pig/
Pigtown) Fromm, Delmar (Denny, as in Dimwit) Edler, and
me. At times we were joined by others but this was the base
cadre and we all learned a great deal about each other and
were almost inseparable. The Greek, Dick Haddad, and I all
ended up serving together again in Korea, Dick and I in "B"
Co. and the Greek in Weapons Co., 1st Battalion 5th Marines.
Del and Willie chose to transfer to the 8th Marines and return
to the Med instead of going to Korea in 1952.

By the spring of 1952 when C-1-6 returned from the
Med, the situation in Korea had stabilized and the demand
for Far East cannon fodder was being met in large part by
Marines graduating from San Diego Recruit Center. These
new Marines were being given a crash course known as ITR
(Infantry Training Regiment), then being sent to the 1st
Division as individual replacements for troops who were
rotating to the States or who had become casualties. The

2nd Division continued to rebuild and, while units to be deployed were at full strength, this was achieved by transferring personnel between regiments.

I make much of having served in the 5th Regiment, and rightly so. It has a rich history and continues to be a first-class fighting force. However, I joined the 5th Marines as a replacement because it was policy at that time to rotate individuals rather than units. I would have been just as proud and at least initially felt a lot more secure to have gone into combat if C-1-6 had been rotated as a unit. We had been together for over a year, were well led and well trained, and most of the regulars had joined to fight. It was only after requesting transfer to the combat theater by letter to the Commandant that some of us were sent to Korea. I regretted leaving some good buddies behind but it was time to find out if I was really a Marine.

```
                          Headquarters              DAE:ghm
                1st Battalion, 6th Marines         1167663
                2d Marine Division, FMF            25 Aug 1952
                   Camp Lejeune, N. C.
```

From: Private First Class David A. EASTON, 1167663/0311 USMC
To: Commandant of the Marine Corps
Via: (1) Commanding Officer, 1st Battalion, 6th Marines
       (2) Commanding Officer, 6th Marines
       (3) Commanding General, 2d Marine Division, FMF

Subj: Transfer, request for

Ref: (a) Paragraph 7016, Marine Corps Manual

1. Reference (a) states that enlisted personnel are afforded
the opportunity, through the medium of official correspondence
to the Commandant of the Marine Corps, via official channels,
to indicate preference of duty station and duty.

2. In accordance with reference (a), it is requested that I
be transferred to the First Marine Division now serving in
Korea.

3. I joined the Marine Corps on 22 January 1951, thinking
that after I had been well trained, I would put the training
to use in a Combat Zone.

4. I have served with the First Battalion, Sixth Marines,
Second Marine Division, FMF, for the past seventeen (17)
months. During this time I have become adequately familiar
with combat tactics and amphibious operations.

5. I am very anxious to have combat experience with the
First Marine Division in Korea.

                                    DAVID A. EASTON

The Fleet Landing

What is a fleet landing? In many port cities it would probably be the name of a waterfront bar. However, to a Marine, it is a place where boats and launches from ships too large or too numerous to tie up to a quay load and/or discharge their passengers.

In Naples, Italy, which was the home port for the U.S. 6th Fleet, ships making this port of call were obliged to drop anchor anywhere from one to three miles offshore. Personnel going ashore from these ships would be ferried to and from the fleet landing. The capital ships, such as aircraft carriers and cruisers, ferried their passengers in launches. These launches were motor driven but other than that looked just like the lifeboats one sees in movies about the sea. The transport to and from the beach for us was less fancy. Unlike the ships of the line, our transport did not have launches. We were shuttled in LCVPs, which are the same boats used to make amphibious landings.

When ships were in port, it was fairly standard to grant liberty to embarked troops and crew members in what was called "port and starboard." This meant 50% were allowed to go ashore and the other 50% remained aboard ship. These privileges were granted on alternate nights between the port and starboard sections. It was also common to have a curfew, usually midnight or 1 a.m., by which time all hands had to be at the fleet landing for the last launch runs to their respective ships.

Fleet landings, regardless of which port or city, could be and often were volatile places. The more ships in a given port, the more volatile the landing areas could be. Contributing factors to this volatility were the rivalries between ships, between the branches of service, and the fueling of these rivalries by the alcohol consumed during the time on the beach. As part of the Marine landing force assigned to the fleet, we Marines preferred fewer ships in port during our visits. A battalion of Marines is right around 1200 men, half of whom might be ashore at any given time. The naval contingent aboard an aircraft carrier was approximately 5000 sailors or 2500 on the beach at the same time. Aircraft carriers did not travel alone so when one pulled into a port there were also swabbies from the cruisers, destroyers, and other accompanying ships let loose in the port of call. Even though there was usually a strong contingent of shore patrol, the Navy's equivalent of MPs in the area of the fleet landing, it could be a tough place at 1 a.m. The best one could hope for was a short wait for the boat going out to his ship and that the rivalries between ships would take precedence to the rivalry between the Navy and the Marines.

There was also a ritual to be observed when the launches, or in our case the LCVPs, arrived back at the ship. When the boat drew alongside there was an angled ladder outside the hull leading up to the quarterdeck. On the quarterdeck stood the OD, or Officer of the Deck. If the flag was flying from the stern of the ship the procedure required each person boarding the ship to face the stern, salute the flag, execute a right facing movement, salute the OD and while saluting request permission to come aboard. If the flag had been lowered then the first part was eliminated. Late at night when a liberty boat pulled alongside, all hands who were mobile and could negotiate the gangplank went aboard and passed by the OD. If there were troops or crew members who were too far gone to make it up the ladder or who were completely passed out, a cargo net was lowered into the boat and they were loaded like cordwood and hoisted to a hatch cover on the main deck. From there, members of their companies were assigned to sort for their own and see that they were taken to their bunks.

A few of my favorite Fleet Landing memories are as follows:

Gus is actually a shortened version of a Polish or Czech name. It belonged to a sailor in the crew of the transport that our company was embarked on. What differentiated Gus from the rest of the crew and most of the sailors in the 6th Fleet was the fact that I had known him in civilian life years earlier. His home in Chicago was less than three blocks from mine.

The incident took place at the top of the gangway late one night as a group of us were returning from a night ashore. Gus was two or three bodies in front of me on the gangplank. He threw the Officer of the Deck a half salute and requested permission to come aboard. The OD returned the salute but remained silent and just stared at Gus intently for probably a full minute. We were in southern Italian waters, it was early in the fall, and the weather was downright balmy. Everyone else was in the uniform of the day, as was Gus, but Gus was also wearing a Navy issue fur-lined deck jacket. Finally the OD told Gus to raise both hands straight up above his head. Gus had no choice but to comply and when he did two bottles of wine, one from under each arm, crashed to the steel deck and broke. The officer of the deck smiled and then said to Gus, "permission to board granted."

On another evening, I was not in the liberty section but was assigned to the deck party to meet the returning boats and assist with the lost souls who couldn't navigate under their own steam. It had been a relatively quiet night without a lot of participation required by the deck party. It was getting late, the last launch had returned and the crew was in the process of raising the LCVPs from the water to their davits where they were normally carried. Another crew was getting ready to raise the gangplank when out of the darkness came a voice, "Don't raise that yet!" There was no sound of a motor to indicate an approaching boat but the voice came again out of the darkness: "Hold the gangplank!" The OD ordered illumination around the ship and there for all to see was a gondola being sculled toward the gangplank ladder. In the gondola was Tony Baldoni, a member of our company. He had missed the last boat from the landing and hired the gondola to bring him out to the ship. Now that he could be seen the next surprise was that Tony was in the uniform of the day but only from the waist up and the ankles down. He had no trousers on. The Officer of the Deck advised Tony that until he was in proper uniform, including trousers, he would not grant him permission to come aboard. One of the Marines in the deck party was in Tony's platoon and while the gondola maintained a position just off the gangway ramp he went below and got Tony a pair of trousers which were lowered over the side to him. Now in the complete uniform of the day, he was given permission to come aboard but then he had to go below and scrounge enough money to go back down the ladder and pay the gondola owner.

Tony was well known in the battalion for his antics and escapades before this incident and it just became another part of the story. No one I know of ever learned what had happened or how Tony lost his pants. All Tony would say was he was glad his ass wasn't still in them. Tony went on to become a professional boxer and was doing pretty well in moving up in the rankings—until he ran into a guy named Tiger Jones. I watched that fight on television and it was the last time I ever saw Tony or heard his name.

The final incident I will relate here took place late at night on the fleet landing in Naples, Italy. There were at least a couple of hundred sailors and Marines waiting on the long concrete pier for rides back to their ships. Being so late there were several in the crowd in a belligerent mood. In particular there was one rather large, black swabbie who was making no secret of the fact that he wanted someone to fight with.

At the end of the pier there was a short concrete wall, perhaps three feet high, to prevent things from going off the pier into the ocean. This sailor had chosen this wall to stand on so he could make himself both heard and conspicuous. He stood there with his back to the ocean and announced in a very loud and contemptuous tone that he was the light heavyweight champion of the 6th Fleet and he could whip any two sailors or any three Marines on this pier and he was ready to prove it. Well somewhere between the words "three Marines" and "prove it," an airborne object became visible. It came out of the crowd with the trajectory of a javelin and was headed straight for the light heavyweight champ of the 6th Fleet. It was a Marine, his right arm was fully extended in front of him, and at the end of his arm was a fist. The fist made contact with the champ's face somewhere in the vicinity of his nose and in sufficient force to knock him over backwards into the sea. There was a loud splash, a chorus of cheers and some laughter. This was followed by a second splash as the Marine's momentum carried him into the ocean as well. I can only assume someone fished both of them out. Our ride to the transport showed up before the episode concluded. I don't know who that Marine was but I would like to buy him a drink. It was a fun thing to behold and even better not to have been involved beyond the spectator stage.

Me & Armand "Blackie" Briere, two BAR men in the boondocks at Camp LeJune

The Scarlet Letter

In the Navy and the Marine Corps, "liberty" is the term used to describe being allowed to go ashore or off base overnight or on weekends. Liberty is not to be confused with leave, which is earned at a rate of 30 days per year. Liberty is a privilege, one that can be denied. Each man had a liberty card, but while on post it was retained in a file in the company office. After hours the cards were in the care of the duty NCO. Individuals wishing to go on liberty were to present their I. D. cards prior to being given their liberty card. The duty NCO was charged with assuring that Marines were squared away and in proper uniform before they were given their liberty cards. The cards in conjunction with an I.D. card acted as passes to the MPs at the gate. Cards were to be returned to the duty NCO upon an individual's return to base.

One evening several of my friends and I decided to go off base for a change of scene and some diversion. For some reason my liberty card was not on file. Of course with me being a private and the duty NCO being a sergeant, it was automatically my fault and I was denied liberty.

The next morning I presented myself in the company office where I spoke with the company clerk. He was a buck sergeant named Brown and, like most clerks, considered himself grossly overburdened. Not coincidentally, he was known to the troops as "Brownie," the nickname having nothing to do with the Girl Scouts.

Brownie reiterated to me that the missing card could

only be a result of my carelessness and that he was too busy to issue a replacement card. He also advised me that even if he wanted to, he could not issue a replacement card without the express permission of the Commandant of the Marine Corps.

Not knowing how or to whom to appeal, I returned to the squad bay in a very depressed mood. Without a liberty card I was a virtual prisoner on the base.

Once word circulated around the platoon, I was paid a visit by two older corporals. Both were reactivated reserves that had seen action in WWII. They were very sympathetic to my plight and suggested I write a letter pleading my case to the Commandant. To be even more helpful, they supplied me with a mailing address.

Knowing that the Commandant was a four star general, I was careful to lace the letter with a lot of "sirs." I also allowed that he was probably a pretty busy guy running the rest of the Corps, so I tried to be brief. The letter left in the next day's mail.

Nothing transpired for a couple of weeks until one day when the company was out in the river practicing rubber boat landings and righting capsized boats. Someone pointed out to me as I was floundering around in the water that I was being paged from shore. The pager was the battalion adjutant and carried the rank of major. He appeared very excited and was jumping up and down and waving a sheaf of papers while yelling my name.

When I reached shore I was proven right. He was very excited. He allowed me to look at the papers he had been waving. On top was my letter to the Commandant. The attachments were endorsements from everyone in the chain of command between the Commandant and me.

After I had reviewed the papers and acknowledged that I had indeed written the letter, I was asked two questions. The first, asked in a very shrill, almost scream, was "Are you insane?" Before I could answer, the major demanded to know, "What kind of fucking nut are you?" Again, before I could form a reply he directed me to get back to the company area and get in the uniform of the day and report to the Sgt. Major. He then added, "On the double. The colonel is waiting to see you!"

When I reported to battalion headquarters, the Sgt. Major marched me directly into the colonel's office. The battalion commander asked me to explain the thought process that took place and resulted in my bypassing the entire chain of command and writing directly to the Commandant.

I informed the colonel of my conversation with Sgt. Brown, the C Company clerk. The colonel dismissed me with the instruction to have the C Company, 1st Sgt. send Sgt. Brown to see the Sgt. Major immediately.

In less than an hour Sgt. Brown sought me out in the barracks and presented me with a new liberty card. For the remainder of my time spent in "C" Company, if for any reason I had to visit the company office, I was treated like a visiting dignitary.

Of course, Sam and Jake, the two reserve corporals who had instigated the whole affair, took all the credit for my new status. As they put it, "Stick with us kid. We'll have you fartin' thru silk."

Bob celebrating Christmas, 1951
aboard the USS Latimer—APA 152
Naples, Italy

Bob

Bob and I first became acquainted in an ROTC class in high school. From our ROTC beginnings a friendship developed which was primarily based on a mutual interest and participation in sports.

Bob's parents were from Mexico and his grandparents still lived there. His home was in Pullman, a neighborhood that consisted of a series of row houses that ran about four blocks north and south, and about an equal distance east to west. These row houses originally served as company housing for the employees of the Pullman Company which built railroad cars in a huge facility that made up the rest of the Pullman neighborhood. There were few young people and even fewer recreational facilities in the Pullman area. As a result, Bob spent a lot of time in West Pullman, which is where I lived, and we played on several of the same sports teams. He was a frequent visitor to and overnight weekend guest in my home. In fact, his visits were frequent enough that over time he began to refer to my parents as Mom and Dad.

I recall being fascinated by what appeared to me to be a complete lack of parental concern about Bob's whereabouts or activities. He was frequently away from home overnight without informing his folks that he was going to be staying elsewhere or advising them when he would be home. Behavior such as this would never have been tolerated by my parents, at least not more than once.

Despite the carte blanche approach to parenthood his folks practiced, Bob was never in trouble inside or outside of school, a boast I could not make.

He was well-liked by everyone who knew him even though he had a somewhat serious nature and was interested in only things athletic. He was also very independent. When I and some of the other guys in our group decided to do something more in keeping with our age group, like chase girls or gamble, he would seldom participate. Instead he would go back to Pullman and hang out in a restaurant where he was a sometime employee. At closing time he and the owner would go to an all night bowling alley on 87th Street and bowl till the wee hours of the morning.

Bob's Mexican heritage was apparent in his appearance. He was a shade darker than most of the guys in West Pullman and had a head of thick black hair. His hairline was low and his eyebrows were very prominent features, so much so that he showed very little forehead. His physique was well-proportioned and he was blessed with excellent coordination and athletic ability. He had an easygoing nature and while he had a sense of humor he rarely was the one to tell a joke. In all the time I knew him, I cannot recall him ever having a dispute of a serious nature with anyone. Following graduation from high school, we both got jobs and saw each other less frequently but continued to play on the same baseball and football teams. In early 1951 Bob called me to let me know he was joining the Marine Corps. Before the call ended I decided I would also join up.

We left Chicago on January 21st for Parris Island. It was our good fortune to be assigned to the same tent all through the 8 weeks of boot camp. Our ROTC training stood us in good stead as we had already learned things like close-order drill, facing movements, and the manual of arms, thereby avoiding a lot of personal attention from the drill instructors—something we learned very quickly to avoid whenever possible.

The only boot camp incident I can recall involving

Bob had to do with the one-size fits-all Marine Corps haircut. Our platoon was marched to the barber shop still wearing our civilian clothes. We were ordered to remove our civvies and package them up for shipment home, or if preferred, to just deep-six them in the provided trash cans. Having completed that task and being stark naked, we were next ordered to get into one of the lines leading to the barber chairs. Following the barber's exercise of his tonsorial artistry, we were funneled into a tunnel-like shower that had a full-length mirror opposite the exit. I followed Bob into the shower and to this day I can still smile at the memory of emerging from the shower to see an absolutely awestruck Bob standing in front of the mirror rubbing one hand back and forth over his scalp wondering where in the hell his hair had gone. It takes longer to tell this than the actual time elapsed because there was a DI posted at the mirror with a belt to keep the line moving and we each got a substantial whack on the ass for slowing down.

From there we got into another line running in front of a counter and set in front of bins containing all manner of military clothing. There was a Marine stationed at each bin and as each recruit stepped in front of him, he would reach into a bin, grab the number of items in the bin that constituted a standard issue of that item and hurl it across the counter in an attempt to knock the recipient down. The challenge was to catch or collect the item or items and stuff them into a sea bag and move to the next bin without slowing down the line. To slow the line down was to incur the wrath of the aforementioned drill instructor who was ready with a belt to accelerate the slower among us.

At the completion of boot camp, Bob and I once again received orders that would see us both go to the same outfit in North Carolina, in fact we were both in the same platoon along with several other members of our recruit graduating class. We served together there for over a year, including a six-month cruise with the 6th Fleet in the Mediterranean Sea. On the cruise I never saw anyone who could get seasick more easily or more violently than Bob. I'm sure everyone has heard the term "he turned green." Well, in Bob's case, with his Mexican complexion, there was no exaggeration with "he turned green." The ship we were aboard was tied up to the quay in Oran, Algeria, and Bob was sleeping peacefully in his rack. One of the guys woke him and inquired why he wasn't seasick. Bob's reply was that as long as we were in port he had no problems. He was then told that the ship had left port while he snoozed. Bob immediately leapt from the rack and headed for the rail only to find on arrival there that we were in fact still tied up. I often suggested to him that his problem was mental, but he would never buy into that.

Not too long after our unit's return from the Med, I left Bob behind when I left the 6th Marines to report to California for training prior to going to Korea. Bob came to Korea a bit later. He ended up assigned as a replacement in an amphibious tractor unit, not great duty for a guy who got seasick aboard much larger craft. An Amtrak in the water was like a cork in the ocean. His unit's job was to patrol the Imjin River, which ran parallel with and to the rear of the Marine front lines. Also, in case of a Chinese breakthrough, all the Imjin bridges would be blown and the Amtrak unit would then become the division's ferry service across the river. I only saw Bob once during our time in Korea, but we did rotate home on the same ship and were discharged on the same day at Treasure Island Naval Station in California.

Our association continued, although not as closely as before. I sponsored Bob to join an athletic club I belonged to. The club sponsored three softball teams and had a football team that played in the South Suburban semi-pro league. I should mention here that between Pullman where Bob lived and West Pullman where I lived there was another neighborhood called Roseland. The Roseland team in the South Suburban League was our archrivals. The first year we were back in Chicago, Bob and I played on the same softball team and we both played on the football team. At the end of the football season Bob was dissatisfied because he had not been given enough playing time. The fact of the matter was that he insisted on being considered for the quarterback position on a team that had won three consecutive league championships with the quarterback currently on the roster.

The following year Bob did not try out for the club team; he instead went to play for the team from Roseland. In those days it was usual for players to play both offense and defense, albeit in different positions depending on who had the ball. Bob made the Roseland squad and got to play quarterback on offense and also was the safety and punt returner on defense. It was tradition for the two local teams to play a benefit game on Thanksgiving Day at a local stadium. It rained all night Thanksgiving eve and there was still a drizzle falling on game day. At kickoff the field had the consistency of oatmeal. This was the first, last, and only time that Bob and I ever participated in a sporting event where we were not on the same side.

After three quarters there was no scoring. Late in the fourth quarter our team had the ball but had to punt from around the Roseland 40-yard line. The kick sailed high into the end zone, where instead of downing the ball Bob caught it and tried to run it out. I was able to get downfield and tackle him in the end zone for a safety, and our team went on to win the game 2-0. As the teams were leaving the field I approached Bob to say a few words, but he refused to speak to me and to this day we have never shared another word. I admit I made no effort to re-establish contact after that. Had I done him a personal injury or in some other way violated our friendship, I would certainly have run him to ground and apologized. I was then and to an extent still am disappointed that years of friendship were cast aside over such a trivial matter.

I can only conclude that both of us had changed considerably over the preceding years and no longer had enough in common to sustain the bond between us. I harbor no ill will toward Bob and would be his friend again in a heartbeat given the chance.

Dick and Bob outside the 6ᵗʰ Marine barracks in Camp LeJeune. Note "Corpsman" Dick is wearing dress shoes.

Dick

I first got to know Dick in boot camp in January of 1951. After boot camp we served together in the 6th Marines thru the rest of 1951 and part of 1952. At that point I was shipped to the Far East where I was assigned to the 1st Bn.5th, "B" Co. Dick followed a month later and ended up in 1st Bn.5th, but in "A" Co.

Dick was tall, thin, quiet, easy-going, and always willing to help a comrade with anything at all. He loved Country & Western music, and at the time he was particularly fond of "Peace in the Valley" by, as best I can remember, either Red Foley or Eddy Arnold. Dick would not stand out in a crowd, but he had a sly side that one would never suspect. I also remember that when something struck him as funny, he would cover his mouth with a loose fist and laugh into his hand.

The sly side of Dick became apparent after we had been in C-1-6 for a while. He was a regular at sick call and after each visit he would return to the barracks with an assortment of remedies in boxes, bottles, and envelopes. He stashed all these medications in the tray of his locker box and as a result was nicknamed "The Corpsman." For the uninitiated, a corpsman is a medical specialist from the Navy, assigned to the Marine Corps, the equivalent of an Army medic—wait! Make that the equivalent of three or four Army medics.

However, his slyness went well beyond collecting

medicines. The training in Charlie Company was both intensive and repetitious, so Dick found a way to avoid the repetition. Somehow he convinced the medical officer that he was not only allergic to just about every plant that grew in North Carolina, but that he also had a foot condition which could not tolerate the standard issue field shoes (called "Boondockers.") The result was that he was not required to spend time in the boondocks or participate in any activity or exercise that required the wearing of field shoes—like conditioning hikes!

Like they say, all good things must come to an end. Late one afternoon the company was returning from an all day hike and the CO wanted to get back to main side at a specific time. We were behind his schedule so he decided to take a short cut across the post golf course. We crossed several fairways on a diagonal and lo and behold, who should be coming down one of them but allergy-riddled PFC Dick. Wearing dress oxfords, of course.

After a few choice words, the skipper had him join the column for the march back to the barracks. Once we hit main side this caused a few raised eyebrows. Here are guys all sweaty, carrying rifles, machine guns, and mortars, and in the ranks is this guy with a flowered shirt and a set of golf clubs on his shoulder. It was the end of Dick's light duty and the day he came back into the Marine Corps.

Another humorous story I recall involves Dick's dad. Our battalion was deployed to the Mediterranean with the 6th Fleet from September 1951 to March 1952. When we got back, several of us from the Midwest took leave and all agreed to meet at Dick's house for a party. There was a good turnout of Marines from Michigan and the northern suburbs of Chicago. Dick's family home had a completely decorated basement where the party took place, and Dick's dad unwittingly supplied the highlight of the evening when he sneezed and sent his false teeth skittering between couples on the dance floor.

Dick's platoon leader in C-1-6 was a 2nd Lt. named Redfield. I didn't know him well, but he had the reputation in his platoon of being kinda "prissy." When I arrived in Korea, I was assigned to "B" Co.5th Marine Regt. As chance would have it, so was Mr. Redfield, who would now be my platoon leader. Dick came over in the next rotation draft and was assigned to the same battalion but to "A" Co. He gave me some flak about my platoon leader, but within a matter of a few days of Dick's arrival, Lt. Redfield was reassigned to "A" Company, and guess who was in his platoon? This situation was short lived though because Mr. Redfield was hit and evacuated and never came back to the unit. He turned out not to be as prissy as thought and was in fact a pretty good combat officer.

From what I have written so far I would guess that Dick might appear as a bit of a goldbrick and not such a good Marine. I trust that what follows may change that view.

In February, 1953 our battalion was on line. "A" Co. was on the left flank and tied in with the 1st Regiment. "B" Co. was in the center and "C" Co. was on the battalion right, tied in with the 3rd battalion 5th Marines. In late February or early March, "A" Company sent out a large combat patrol (a diesel, in radio code) whose objective was to search for and destroy encountered enemy forces. Dick was a member of this patrol. The diesel had proceeded well into no-man's land in their search for gooks to beat up on, but this time Luke the Gook got there first and had an almost perfect ambush set up. The enemy's well-coordinated initial burst of fire either killed or incapacitated all but two members of the patrol. One was a Marine from Hawaii who had been wounded in both legs. The other was Dick. These two took shelter behind a rice paddy dike and returned fire.

The initial outburst could be heard from the MLR and raised the alarm that the patrol was engaged. Attempts to make radio contact yielded no result, so as was usual in such cases a relief column was formed and put on standby. These relief formations were referred to as "angels." Sending out angels was always a risky thing to do because it was a page in the Chinese playbook to cut off a unit and then ambush the relief, which was sure to come. This is what happened when the angels were dispatched. They held their own but were unable to break through and reach the ambush site.

The sounds reaching the MLR clearly indicated a very one-sided battle was in progress. The rapid "brrrt-brrrt" of numerous Chinese burp guns and the heavier and very distinctive report of a single BAR answering in short bursts provided a scenario of what was taking place. All of this was punctuated from time to time by the detonation of grenades. After each explosion or series of burp-gun fire, the Marines on the line would hold their breath, waiting for the BAR response. Each time the response came, and we would all hope that whoever the gunner was, he was hitting the mark. This went on for several hours until finally the sky began to lighten and the Chinese, in fear of air support and increased visibility of artillery spotters, abandoned the field. The angels arrived at the scene, where they found Dick—the Marine manning the BAR—and the wounded kid from Hawaii loading magazines and scrounging ammo from the nearest casualties.

For the night's work, Dick collected numerous small grenade fragment wounds to his hands and face. In addition he had three furrows from burp gun slugs cut into the outside of his upper left arm just below the shoulder of his flak jacket. But the most amazing thing of the evening was his helmet. Front and center about two inches above the rim was a jagged hole where a bullet had exited from inside the helmet. The slug had gone in under the rim, passed completely around his head, burning off the hair in its passage, and exited above his forehead. Dick brought the helmet home and it must stir deep memories for him when he looks at it.

A couple of months after the firefight I was given an up close and personal example of this guy's grit. Our battalion was in reserve and it was common practice to organize "smokers" between units. These would be called boxing matches by civilians. Being about the same size, it was determined by the draw that Dick would fight for "A" Co. and I would represent "B" Co. It may sound immodest but I was a much better boxer than Dick. This became apparent at the opening bell, but no matter how much punishment he took, he just kept coming. Having been his friend for so long and holding him in high esteem for his actions under fire, it was very difficult to hit him, but it was also a matter of survival. There was just no quit in him and while I won the bout there was no satisfaction in the victory.

After our discharges in late 1953, we both returned to the Chicago area. I was working at 22nd Street and Dick had a job in the city. We would see each other occasionally on the commuter train. Eventually I was moved to the night shifts, stopped riding the train, and lost contact with Dick. I regret this now because he was a good Marine, a good person, and had been a good friend over a tough stretch. Wherever he may be, I wish him well.

*This is J.P. Ever seen a more "Gung Ho"
Marine?*

J.P.

If there were such a thing as a stereotypical Marine, few people would pick J.P. out of a crowd to fit the stereotype. He was not an imposing physical specimen, and one of the last adjectives a casual acquaintance would apply to him was "tough." He was a roly-poly little guy with a quick smile, a soft voice, and a gracious manner to everyone. There was a trace of New York in his speech, and if you were to guess he was of Irish descent, you would win a cigar. He was blessed with a wonderful tenor singing voice, loved to sing, and knew the words to every Irish song ever written. I attribute my extreme fondness for the song "Danny Boy" to J.P. It is not only a beautiful melody that tells a great story, it conjures up many a memory from a good time in my life.

It is difficult to describe just what it was about J.P. that keeps him in mind after so many years. If you needed something, he had it. If you were sad, he would cheer you up. If you were in trouble, he would help. The best definition I can come up with for J.P. would be, "good friend."

When we had our parties in the barracks on paydays, he was the chief organizer and bartender. Sometimes before lights out he would entertain by singing. If you were around him long enough you almost felt like you were part Irish, too. He really shone off base. Our group would seek out places that had music, our favorite being a piano bar. Usually there weren't many servicemen as customers in these places, mostly because the price of drinks more often than not was higher than at some of the more popular joints. With J.P.'s voice, this was not a problem for us. He would sing, the civilians would buy drinks, and we, his parasitic friends, would do the rest. I remember a few times in California when it was hard to see the top of the piano thru the bottles and glasses accumulated there.

After being together for a year and a half in the 6th Marines, we both ended up in the 5th Regiment in Korea. He was in Dog Company, 2nd Battalion, and I was in the 1st Battalion, Baker Company. We saw each other from time to time, but one meeting that took place at the end of March 1953 stands out in my memory. My squad had been shuttling casualties from other companies into the aid station on the reverse slope of our hill. This was two or three days into the battle to retake the outpost called Vegas, and all the aid stations were overflowing. I found J.P. sitting on his helmet leaning back against the sandbag wall of the aid bunker. He had his canteen in one hand and a cigarette in the other and looked plumb tuckered out.

He related to me what his outfit had just gone thru in an unsuccessful bid to drive the gooks from the hilltop. Vegas had been overrun on the night of the 26th by a vastly superior number of Chinese. The outpost was 1300 yards from our lines and the Chinese had every inch of ground between the MLR and Vegas zeroed in. In order to counterattack, it was necessary to move forward through a rain of artillery and mortar shells, mostly large caliber. Relief only came when a point was reached where you were close enough to the Chinese lines that the barrage might endanger their own troops. Of course reaching this point put you within range of the defenders machine guns, small arms, and depending on how close you got, maybe hand grenades. J.P. told me that once his platoon reached the far end of the gauntlet of exploding artillery and flying shrapnel, the guys came to port arms and scrambled up the hill toward the gooks. After the 122's and 82's, the small arms stuff whizzing by was almost inconsequential. They got within a hundred yards of the enemy trenches but had taken so many casualties getting there they lacked the manpower and momentum to go all the way to the top. Also, since Vegas was closer to the Chinese held hills than to our lines, it was less difficult for the Chinese to reinforce. The remaining Dog Company force set up a base of fire and assisted the company trying to reach their position. Once the other Company was in position, Dog was relieved and ordered to collect their casualties and return to the MLR. What's ironic about this is that on the night of the 26th when this party started, the 2nd Battalion was in regimental reserve to rest up after a tour on line. When this turned into a serious engagement they were called forward to replace decimated 1st and 3rd Battalion units and to provide warm bodies for a counterattack effort. Before this scrape ended, part of the 7th Marine Regiment was called out of division reserve and participated in the fight also. J.P. was unhurt but it was pretty apparent that he had had enough for one day.

Over the years I have seen J.P. only once. I went to a division reunion at the Waldorf Astoria Hotel in New York City a few years after we served together. I discovered J.P. in the 5th Regiment's hospitality suite. He had me cancel my hotel accommodations and made me a guest at his home on Long Island for the remaining days of the reunion. I recall his mom's name being Bridget and her treating me as a second son. Since then I have spoken to him on the phone on a number of occasions. He went to work for the Postal Service after his discharge. Whenever business took me to New York, I tried to call him.

Regrettably, with the passage of time I have lost contact with J.P. As I wrote earlier there was nothing special about him, he was just an all-around good guy. He was a person anyone would be pleased and proud to have for a friend. I also wrote earlier that he didn't match the stereotype of a Marine, but he was a Marine and a damned good one at that. I was honored and proud to have known and served with J.P. and as long as I can sing "Danny Boy" in the shower he will never be forgotten. Semper Fi, Sean Patrick.

*The Greek. I would hope that at some
point in life everyone could have at least
one friend like him.*

The Greek

His given name was John, but I have no recollection of anyone ever addressing him that way. To other Marines he was just "Greek." I learned later that at home he was known as "Junie," which was his family's version of Junior. When I first met him, Greek was 25 or 26 years old, which made him about six or seven years older than the average trooper in our outfit.

Greek's charm was not in his physical appearance. His hair was dirty-blond and stringy. His top front teeth were a bridge, and, dentistry being what it was in the late 1940's, it was obvious the teeth were not original equipment. His complexion had a rough quality, as if there may have been a go-around with acne during his early teen years. Stature-wise Greek stood right at six feet tall and his shoulders, while not extremely broad, were very square and gave the impression of being broader than they were. The rest of his physique, however, looked like a collection of spare parts. If you have ever seen the movie *Gunga Din,* and can recall how Sam Jaffe, who portrayed Din, looked standing at attention, then you have a fair idea of what I'm talking about.

I first became acquainted with Greek through his friendship with Dave G., who was one of the 5 other guys assigned to my six-man tent in boot camp. Dave G. and Greek had enlisted together and were from the same town north of Chicago. Greek was a frequent visitor to our tent in off-duty hours

At the end of boot camp a large number of our graduating class, including Greek and I, were sent to the 6th Marine Regiment. We were both assigned to the same platoon of "Charlie" Company, but to different squads. We would serve together in C-1-6, until mid-1952, when we both received orders to the 1st Marine Division, which was serving in Korea at that time. Again, we were both assigned to the 1st Battalion, 5th Regiment. Greek went to the 81MM Mortar Section of Weapons Co. and I was sent to "B" or "Baker" Company.

It was during our time in the 6th Marines that our friendship was cemented. Within our platoon six or seven of us formed a social group and Greek was unquestionably the leader. He introduced all of us to a fictional character named "Shel Scott." Shel had been a Marine before becoming a private eye in the mold of Mike Hammer. No question about it, Shel was one cool, tough guy, and I realize now that in many ways Greek wanted to be just as cool and tough as Shel.

In addition to a sense of humor without boundaries, Greek had a talent for music. He played a pretty fair harmonica and I recall being impressed because his harmonica had a plunger on the end that allowed him to hit flats and sharps, or something like that. It wasn't just the plunger that impressed me, but the fact that he seemed to know when to use it. He was also the group song leader and was always organizing a sing-a-long of his favorite tunes, such as "Blue Moon," "Deep Purple," and "Sentimental Journey." When there was one available he could also pound a piano pretty well.

One of my early boot camp recollections of Greek happened on a cold, clear South Carolina night. Greek was on fire watch, patrolling the street between our two rows of parallel tents. It was about two in the morning when he shook me awake and said I had to come outside. I knew I was not on the fire watch schedule, but his voice had a note of urgency in it, so I got out of the sack and stepped into the street. When I did, he said, "Look at that!" I looked around, saw nothing, and asked, "What?" He pointed to the end of the street and said, "Look! A Carolina Moon!" Cold, shivering, and annoyed at being awakened, I asked him, "What the fuck do you expect, we're in Carolina!" then I looked. The just rising moon appeared to be at ground level at the end of the street. It was so broad that its circumference spanned the tents on both sides of the street. It had an orange cast to it and was the biggest, brightest, fullest moon I had ever seen. I know I didn't fully appreciate what I was seeing at the moment but looking back in time I'm glad he woke me. I often think of Greek when I see a particularly full or bright moon, but in all the years that have elapsed since then I have never seen another moon that could compare to that one.

Another Greekism had to do with smoking. I didn't smoke at the time, but watching this happen time after time to the same guys always made me wonder why they didn't catch on. One of the guys would have a cigarette going and Greek would ask for a drag. When they passed him the cigarette, he would take a monster drag that added about a half inch of ash to the end of the butt. Seeing that and knowing that the cigarette was not going to taste very good after that, they often told him to keep it. He did. Only Big Steve ever caught on. He would give Greek an unlit cigarette with the admonition, "You ain't screwin' up my smoke."

One evening in Naples, Italy, our regular group was gathered at the bar in a nightclub. I'm not sure how it all began but an argument started between a sailor and Greek. Stepping into his Shel Scott persona, Greek proposed to the sailor that they settle this man-to-man but in a more dignified manner than just a barroom brawl. Each of them was to get one free punch at the other guy and the loser would buy the winner a drink. A coin was flipped to see who would go first and Greek lost. The sailor's swing landed right on Greek's chin and sent him asshole over tea kettle into some unoccupied chairs. Well, Greek got up, put on what I am sure was a forced smile, and already tasting the free drink he was going to win, swaggered in his best Shel Scott fashion back to the bar. To the swabbie's credit, he played by the rules and waited for what was to come. Greek took his best shot and his punch landed right on the sailor's jaw. His head snapped back, his hat fell to the floor behind him, and that was it. One free drink for the Navy and weeks of derision for Greek.

Another of our ports-of-call was Oran, Algeria. Here we came into contact with quite a number of French Foreign Legionnaires. As I recall there were not many Frenchmen in the ranks, mostly Germans. There had recently been several movies about the Foreign Legion in circulation, *Beau Geste* being the most notable. Typical of Greek, this captured his imagination and he began soliciting the group to consider that when our hitch was up in the Corps, we would all come back to Oran and sign up in the Legion. I was the only one who paid him the slightest attention and the next thing I know he is presenting me with two copies of a contract that he has drawn up, one for each of us. To make it official and binding, he insisted that it had to be signed— in blood! I held out for a plain old signature. We compromised at a signature in ink and an accompanying "X" in blood after our names. Obviously this contract was never executed, but I still have my copy in a scrapbook.

When our convoy pulled into the harbor that serves as the seaport for Athens, Greece, Greek and I along with two other Marines hit the beach armed with the name and address of the brother of Greek's father. We figured it would be easy to look him up in a phone book, but we had not factored in the Greek alphabet. After hitting several dead-ends in our search, we were fortunate enough to recognize a Bell System logo on the front of a building. In we went and found out it was the main telephone exchange for Athens and there were English speaking people working there. They proved most helpful in locating Greek's uncle, or I should say in helping Greek's uncle to locate us. The operator who tracked him down told us to wait in front of the building and his uncle would be there shortly.

In less than 15 minutes a chauffer-driven limousine

pulled up and Mr. K. got out to meet the nephew he had never seen. It seems Greek's uncle was the head man at the largest textile mill in Greece, and the limo was his normal mode of transport. We learned later that he also traveled a bit by boat because his residence was on an island he owned just off shore. We piled into the limousine and were taken on a personally guided tour of Athens which included the Acropolis and the Parthenon.

Later we were taken to a very upscale restaurant for dinner. I don't recall what I had to eat, but I was really impressed when the bill was presented and no money changed hands. Mr.K. just signed his name and away we went. A lot of eyebrows went up when the limo dropped off four enlisted Marines at the fleet landing where we caught a launch back to our ship. Following this excursion Greek was able to get a 72-hour pass and spend the time with his uncle on the island.

Upon our return from the Mediterranean, Greek decided to get married. He wanted to be married in dress blues and asked Big Steve and me to be in his wedding party. The wedding was to be held in his hometown. For personal reasons, Big Steve had to decline. Under normal circumstances planning a wedding can be complex. When Greek was involved nothing was normal. All of us being infantrymen, we had never been issued dress blues. We were able to find a couple of guys who had previously been on sea duty and borrowed their blues. The next obstacle was that neither of us had enough cash to fly roundtrip from North Carolina, and on top of that we could only get seven days leave. By pooling our money we were able to get Greek a one-way ticket to Chicago. I was able to catch a ride with a couple of guys as far as Beaver Falls, Pennsylvania, and hitchhiked across Ohio and Indiana to my parents' house. The plan was for me to show up at Greek's house the day before the wedding, and after the wedding and a one day honeymoon, he would use some of the money he expected to get as wedding gifts to buy us both a return flight back to camp in time for roll call Monday morning

Right on schedule I showed up with my dress blues on a hanger the day before the wedding. The rehearsal went off without a hitch. The next day I went to his house about an hour before we were to leave for the ceremony. It was then I learned that instead of carrying his borrowed uniform home with him he had shipped it—and it had not arrived. Everyone else was in their tuxedos and Greek was in his underwear sitting at the piano, playing "Blue Moon" and smoking a cigar. Fortunately, someone had the foresight to order an extra tux and as it turned out I wore the tuxedo and Greek was married in the dress blues that had hitchhiked home with me.

The wedding and reception went smoothly enough and I left with the agreement to meet Greek at the airport Sunday afternoon for the trip back to base. I should have known better . . . .

Sunday morning I got a call from the newlywed and he had decided to extend his honeymoon another day. Plan B was that he would meet me at the airport Tuesday instead of Sunday. With some trepidation I arrived at the airport Tuesday, and lo and behold there was Mr. and Mrs. Greek, with two airplane tickets in hand. We arrived at the main gate of camp quite late Tuesday night. I half expected the MP's at the gate to pull us off the bus as deserters, but they passed us thru.

At Wednesday morning's roll call it only took the gunny a moment to spot Greek in the front rank and immediately call him out of formation. As soon as Greek stepped forward I became visible and was also called out of ranks. We were instructed to get into the uniform of the day and stand by for office hours with the colonel. Once dressed, we were sent to the sergeant major's office to await the colonel's pleasure. Greek was marched in to present himself and I was told to wait in the hall outside the office. After fifteen or twenty minutes had passed, Greek came out and said, "Let's go." Remembering how I got to this point in the first place I was not about to walk away from an appointment with the battalion commander on Greek's say so. A few minutes later the sergeant major came out and said, "You can go."

*Greek returning from a landing excercise
during the Med cruise*

*Dick Haddad, Wally Day, Mr. Kyritsi (Greek's uncle),
Greek, and me during our tour of Athens.*

Greek with an 81mm mortar in early 1953

Greek taking life easy in corps reserve, May 1953

As we walked back to the company area Greek filled me in. We had both been placed on restriction to the immediate area until we received and presented confirmation from the airline that we in fact had reservations which would have gotten us back to base on time and that such reservations had been cancelled. That evening we spent several hours crafting a very carefully composed letter to the airline hoping it would draw a response acceptable to the colonel. In a week or so a letter arrived addressed to Greek that verified that reservations had been held in our names for Sunday, but had been cancelled and rebooked for Tuesday. The letter made no mention of the fact that the cancellation and rebooking had been done at our request. The letter was taken to the sergeant major for delivery to the colonel. Later that day we were notified that our restriction was lifted and no entries would be made in our service records of the incident.

I must have learned something from this because later when we were in California just before sailing for overseas, Greek and I were in an all-night hash house having breakfast in the wee hours of a Monday morning. He decided he was going to spend the day in San Diego, and that as an infantryman on his way to Korea there wasn't an awful lot the Corps could do about it. I sat on the curb in front of the restaurant with him for half an hour trying to talk him out of staying but he wasn't listening. I got back to camp for roll call and Greek showed up late that night. His punishment was being assigned as the gunny's personal valet on the ship crossing the Pacific. His duties included sitting on a bucket next to the gunny's sack and playing the harmonica.

After our arrival in Korea, I didn't see much of Greek for a while. Even though we were in the same battalion, the 81mm mortars had a range of almost 6000 yards and were usually sited one or two ridgelines behind the letter companies whom they supported. It so happened that when the 5th Marines came back on line in late January of 1953, the 81's were situated behind the next hill from the one occupied by "B" Company and adjacent to the main supply road. As a result, whenever I was able to shake loose for a shower or go to the rear for any other reason, I would pass right through their position.

On my first visit to the 81 site, I stopped at a gun pit and asked a couple of mortar men if they could point out the Greek's bunker. They showed me where it was but advised caution if I intended to enter. As I approached I could hear what could only be gunshots coming from within. I paused and announced myself at the entryway and was rewarded with a "Come on in!" Inside Greek was lying on his back with one hand across his chest holding a .45 automatic. He had been shooting at rats as they scurried along between the timbers that formed the support for the roof of the bunker. He was not wearing his boots and the bottoms of his socks had a light reflecting crust that was probably between an eighth and a quarter-inch thick. I asked him when he was going to shit-can those socks. He told me that he was going to wear them home and have taps put on the heels and toes. He just wasn't sure if they would ever take a good spit shine.

The Chinese really did not like the 81's at all. They spent a lot of time searching for them with their own mortars of the 82 and 120 mm variety. As fate would have it a small piece of shrapnel from one of these probing bursts found its way to Greek's ass. There's an old axiom in the Marine Corps, that if you are looking for sympathy it can be found in the dictionary: it's between shit and syphilis. All Greek ever got from his friends was being asked to explain how a guy gets hit in the ass if he's facing the gooks.

When the 1st Marine Division went into corps reserve it was like old home week. Big Steve had come overseas and was assigned to "B" Company, so he was just two tents down in the same row as my tent. Weapons Company was bivouacked across the road and Greek's tent was about fifty yards from mine. The three of us got to spend a lot of time together. Once we went back on line and after the ceasefire we rarely saw Greek until we assembled in Ascom City for the trip home.

Greek's family was in the restaurant business. His uncle

was the owner, his dad was the chief cook, and his mom was the cashier. This was no small scale operation. Their specialty was fish and the restaurant had its own fleet of fishing trawlers which plied Lake Michigan daily to insure the freshness of the servings. Junie, as he was known there, liked to tell the story about his Pop. When a patron would request "something without bones," the old man would say, "For cryssa sake! This is a seafood place. Give the sumanabitch pancakes!"

After we had returned to civilian life I would occasionally drive up and visit on a weekend. The first couple of trips Junie was tending bar in the restaurant lounge. This was good for me because I could sit at the bar and we could talk in his free moments. On a subsequent visit there was a new bartender on duty. I asked if it was Greek's night off and was told that he was now working in the kitchen. When I entered, Greek was putting a lobster order under the warming light to wait for waitress pick-up. In addition to the sprig of parsley adorning the plate, the lobster was holding a lit, half-smoked cigarette in one of its pincers. Greek explained to me how he came to be working in the kitchen: His uncle told him that for every five bottles of scotch that he bought, he was only selling two and Junie was drinking three.

Early in 1954, Big Steve asked Greek and me to be in his wedding party. The wedding was to take place in a town just north of Detroit. I was working the four-to-midnight shift and usually arrived at the house about 12:45 a.m. A couple of nights before the ceremony was to take place I arrived to find Greek sitting at the kitchen table with my mom and dad. They were having a great time. I got cleaned up, packed a bag, and Greek and I were off into the night headed for Detroit.

It was close to 4 a.m. when we passed a sign in southern Michigan that said "Paw-Paw." I casually mentioned to Greek that Paw-Paw was the home of another Marine that we had known in Charlie-One-Six and in Baker-One-Five. That's all it took. In a matter of moments we were in downtown Paw-Paw and Greek was on the phone telling Willie we would pick him up in fifteen minutes and that we were all going to a wedding. Willie was game and we picked him up and continued on our way. We arrived safely, the wedding went very well, and a good time was had by all.

In 1957 I reenlisted in the Marine Corps and haven't seen Greek since about a year before that. Indirectly I heard that life has not been good to Greek. On a business trip to New York in the 80's, I called another old friend, J.P., and he told me that Greek showed up at his front door in the early hours one morning. He said he learned that Greek was divorced and unemployed and added that Greek looked like shit. Greek had no plans, and at that moment, he was just traveling around visiting any of his old service buddies that he could find. It's possible he may have tried to find me also, but between the service and my job I was a moving target in those days.

I can recall on several occasions hearing Greek describe how he wanted to leave this world. He would be standing on the crest of a hill with a pearl-handled revolver in each hand heroically holding off swarms of an enemy. Of course, in Greek's version of this, there would be an American flag flying just behind him and the Marines Hymn would be playing in the background and somehow this whole scene would be captured on film.

I was truly sorry to hear about Greek's bad luck. I guess if there was one thing I could give him it would be the two pearl-handled pistols and the chance to end his days according to his vision. I know he would have liked that. Shel Scott would approve also.

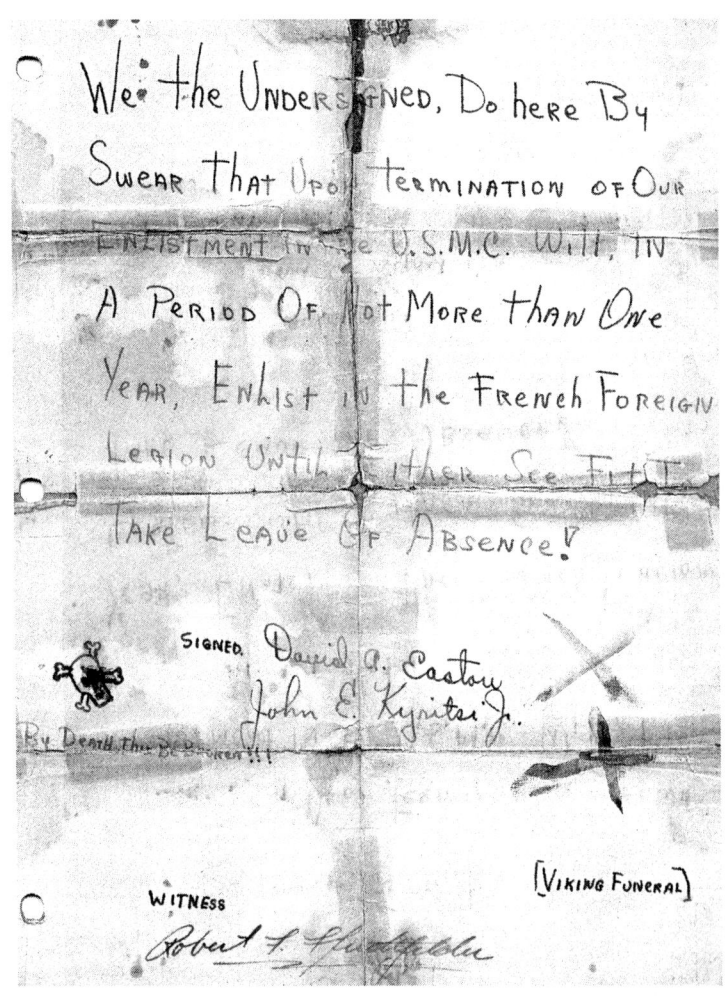

We: the UNDERSIGNED, Do here By Swear That Upon termination of Our ENLISTMENT in the U.S.M.C. Will, IN A PERIOD OF Not More thAN One Year, ENList iN the French FOREIGN Legion Until I Ether See Fit T TAKE Leave of ABSENCE!

SIGNED, David A. Easton

John E. Kyritsi Jr.

By Death they Departed!!!

[VIKING FUNERAL]

WITNESS

Robert F. _____

The Foreign Legion contract drawn up by John "The Greek" Kyritsi, duly signed but still unfulfilled as of this writing.

Anthony P. Douglas, better known as Doug.
If I told you what the initial P stands for he
would hunt me down and hurt me.

Doug

I had been in the service seven months when I first met Doug. He and one other Marine transferred into the 6th Marines as part of the build-up of manpower prior to our departure for the Mediterranean. He was a slick-sleeve private when he joined our platoon. That was usually an indicator of a run-in with higher authority. I only got to know him casually during the cruise but later we became good friends.

In the early days of our acquaintance I was not sure I would ever want to be a friend of his, but I do have to say that I was fascinated by his approach to life. I have never known anyone who lived more in the moment than Doug. He never visibly worried about things for more than ten or fifteen minutes. His philosophy seemed to be, "yesterday is over with, tomorrow hasn't come yet, so let's do something now."

He was of Puerto Rican descent and had what is commonly called an olive complexion with wavy black hair and a quick, mischievous smile. His 190 pounds was well distributed over a 6-foot muscular frame. He was quick-witted and possessed a well-developed sense of humor that had a definite tilt to the bawdy side.

There is no way I could convince myself that Doug was an ultra-squared away garrison Marine. Yes, his shoes had a shine (albeit low luster), his weapon passed inspection, and he could stay in step during close order drill. It was his antics in the barracks and during off-duty hours that set him apart and frequently got him into hot water. Despite all that, he was definitely the guy you wanted in the foxhole with you when the feces collided with the oscillator.

The first of Doug's escapades that I recall took place while we were anchored in Naples, Italy. He and I were BAR men in the same platoon but in different squads. When in ranks, his position in the formation was directly in front of me. We were in ranks on the deck one morning for a weapons inspection by our company commander when I got the first indication that something had transpired between Doug and the CO.

When the CO executed his left face and came directly in front of Doug, the CO burst out laughing, did a right face and moved on to the next man. The night before the inspection had been a liberty night for us, and our CO had been acting as a shore patrol officer on the beach. The SP's routinely dropped in unannounced at establishments that had been declared off limits to U.S. military personnel. Whorehouses fell into that category and during a visit to one such place of business the SP's burst in to find a buck-naked Doug. When he recognized our CO he jumped to attention. The skipper also recognized Doug as one of his own and gave him a lecture about being in an off-limits facility. He was told to get dressed and get out of there, which he did.

Not too much later in the evening the shore patrol visited a different bordello where they must have believed they were experiencing déjà vu. There in front of the CO stood a very naked Doug, trying to explain his presence in what he knew to be an off-limits site. This time the lieutenant took a sterner line. He confiscated Doug's liberty card and ordered him back to the ship. That should have been the end of the incident, but if you believe that, you didn't know Doug.

At a third house of ill repute later that evening the whole scenario was reenacted yet again. This time the skipper assigned a member of the shore patrol to take Doug to the fleet landing and to stay with him until he boarded a launch back to our ship. I later overheard the CO tell our platoon leader that he would never again be able to look at Doug without visualizing him naked, at attention, with a big hard-on.

It was after returning from the Med that I got to know Doug better. On paydays a group of us used to throw in a few bucks and instead of going out to the slop chute or the local honky tonks, one of our number would take a bus to the ABC store in Jacksonville and bring back some sippin' stuff. All of our sergeants were brown-baggers and gone for the evening. We would put on some music, set up a bar on a couple of locker boxes, light a few candles and sit there well into the next morning shooting the shit about all kinds of important stuff. Doug was the most frequent courier, mostly because his age made him a legal buyer in the ABC store and secondly the risk of smuggling contraband liquor past the MPs at the gate never seemed to bother him. It was during these late night sessions that Doug and I decided that we had trained long enough and that we should be in the 1st Marine Division. There had been a recent solicitation for volunteers to transfer to the 8th Regiment, as they were building up troop levels prior to their tour in the Mediterranean. Of our group, only two guys opted for this offer. Within the next couple of months the rest of the group were all in possession of orders to the Far East. Doug and I were the first to leave and the others followed. Two of these friends actually ended up in the same Company with me in Korea.

When Doug and I arrived in California, we were assigned to the same squad. Other than the platoon sergeant and Doug and I, there were only two other infantry Marines in the platoon. The four of us were designated as a fire team and invariably were on point for every field exercise. We looked pretty good climbing those hills in front of a bunch of clerk typists and motor pool guys but those damned hills almost did us in after our time in the swamps of North Carolina.

Pickle Meadows was the name given to a remote part of the Sierra Madre Mountains where we were taken for a couple of weeks of cold weather training. There was a cadre of veterans of the fighting in Korea stationed there. They acted in place of the enemy, emulating Chinese tactics. Along with making life miserable for us in general, they also had an objective of taking prisoners whenever possible. The Chinese put great effort into taking prisoners for the propaganda value of doing so.

It was common practice that whenever we halted, the unit would assume a defensive perimeter. In addition, if it was after dark we would also dig in just as if we were in an actual combat situation. Early one morning well before sunrise we were awakened to the clash of cymbals, whistles being blown, and the blare of trumpets. Within moments our perimeter had been overrun by a cadre frontal assault. Any Marine touched before he cleared his sleeping bag was declared KIA. They also worked in pairs to grab an individual and drag him off as a prisoner. Two of them made an error in judgment. They decided to drag Doug off the hill. Before it was over they were our prisoners and both required medical treatment, one with a broken nose. Doug was back in his sleeping bag before the corpsman finished working on the guy's nose.

Another typical Doug story relates to a weekend liberty he and I took in Tijuana, Mexico with the other two Marines in our fire team. It all started out pretty well. We had some Mexican chow and spent several hours at the local jai alai fonton. We met some American tourists there and they insisted on buying us several rounds of drinks. Later, much later, we were in a Mexican cantina below street level. Other than us and a solitary sailor at the bar, there were no other Americans in the place. Doug and I were at that stage of the evening where we knew with the absolute certainty possessed only by the inebriated that we were sober. By comparison to our two companions, we were. They both had their heads down on the table, and whether you call it asleep or passed out the description applied. I was babysitting at the table and Doug had disappeared out on the dance floor. I heard a commotion behind me from the direction of the dance floor and the first thing I noticed was the sailor heading for the exit. Doug appeared and suggested that we leave, fast!

With that, he hoisted Geno onto his shoulder and headed for the exit. I managed to get Al on his feet with one of his arms over my shoulder and one of my arms around his back. We, too, headed for the exit. To reach street level after leaving the bar it was necessary to climb 5 or 6 stairs. We were halfway to the top when two Mexicans the size of NFL defensive tackles appeared on the sidewalk. One of them was wearing brass knuckles and the other had his hand in the side pocket of his suit coat. The guy with his hand in his pocket said "OK gringo, now we finish what you start!" Without the slightest pause Doug replied, "We don't fight that way. There are four of us and only two of you. Go get a couple of more Mexicans." I knew I could run faster if I just dropped Al, but Doug and his burden were blocking the stairway. Then "God Bless the Navy," the little swabbie who had run from the bar showed up with two Mexican policemen in tow. The two bruisers disappeared and the policemen put us in a van and took us to the border, where they turned us over to a couple of gung-ho Marine MPs. These stiffs were not going to let us pass because Al was not wearing his cover. In a less than coherent manner, Al advised them that he had no fucking idea where his cover was. After we finally were allowed to cross the border I ragged on Al all the way back to camp about losing his cover. When we got to the tent and I unbuttoned my jacket, Al's cover fell out. I had put it inside my jacket in the cantina so Al wouldn't lose it. It was good to be back in our own country alive and well.

There occurred one other incident while we were still in California. I don't recall what Doug did but it incurred someone's wrath and he found himself restricted to the post for the weekend to come. At the time we were back at San Onofre, a tent camp in the hills near Camp Pendleton. We were billeted in six-man tents that had wooden decks. Friday night came and Al, Geno, and I were heading for San Diego. We were sorry Doug couldn't come but not to the point of giving up one of our last few weekends in the States before shipping out.

It was pitch dark when we returned and made our way down the road between the two parallel rows of tents. As we neared our tent there appeared to be some sort of glow coming from it. I drew back the flap and stepped up onto the wooden floor. Only problem with that move was that there was no floor and I almost pitched forward into the tent. When I recovered I saw Doug sitting on the edge of his cot, with a half-empty case of beer and a small fire burning at his feet. The fire was being fueled by the floor of the tent, which Doug had torn up and split into kindling with his trusty entrenching tool. That's the same entrenching tool he used to pry the hasp off the storage area at the enlisted men's club so he could get the beer. He'd been a busy guy while we were gone and was feeling no pain at the moment. He promised not to burn the tent down so we all hit the sack. He wanted to finish the beer before he quit for the night.

The platoon sergeant took one look at Doug at the morning formation and told me to get him out of the area before the lieutenant showed up. We walked over to the area where the camp's permanent staff was billeted and went into their mess hall and drank coffee most of the morning. I was amazed because nothing was ever said about the disappearing floor and I think they just wrote off the case of beer, glad the storeroom had not been emptied I suppose. It's probably fortunate that he didn't think about the motor pool or he might have borrowed a truck and made a real haul. He wasn't at all worried about the possible implications if he were brought up on charges. His philosophy was, "I'm an infantryman on my way to Korea. What can they do to me that would be worse than that?"

I just recalled something else. He had a way of referring to himself as "Ol' Dougie." A person could be offering him a drink or inviting him outside to settle a difference of opinion and the answer would more than likely be "never let it be said that Ol' Dougie was one to refuse."

The second day we were in Korea, we were split up with a handshake and a "Good Luck." Doug went to the 7th Marine Regiment and I was assigned to the 5th Marines. We didn't see each other very often but everyone knew which units were on line and how they were faring. Fox Company 2/7 always seemed to be in the thick of things. Through the grapevine I heard about a patrol action in which Doug was involved. He was a buck sergeant by then.

It was a large enough patrol to have a second lieutenant in command. Smaller patrols were usually led by a sergeant. In any case, the patrol made contact in no-man's land with a numerically superior Chinese force and a ferocious firefight broke out. The lieutenant came unglued and Doug took over command. After establishing a covering force he directed the withdrawal and the evacuation of casualties. The patrol was also bringing in two gook prisoners. Doug was assisting a wounded Marine and as they stepped around a "dead" goonie on the paddy dike, the corpse rolled into the rice paddy and placed a concussion grenade on the path. Amazingly the grenade did little more than make noise and Doug immediately remedied the dead gook situation. During this moment of chaos, the other two prisoners thought to escape. In a sense they did avoid captivity. They joined their comrade wherever those guys went when a Marine cancelled the rest of their enlistment.

When I said the 7th Marines always seemed to be in the thick of things, it was true. Early in March of 1953 the 1st Marines relieved the 7th on line and the regiment went into division reserve for a well-earned rest. By the end of March, the 7th had been ordered forward as a counterattack force in the battle for the outposts Reno, Carson, and Vegas. Carson was held and Reno was lost, but Vegas was contested by both sides non-stop for four days. The 5th Marine regimental reserve had been committed and so the 7th was called up to continue the battle. Ultimately the Chinese were driven off and it was Fox 2/7 that regained the crest on the fourth day.

A month or so later the entire 1st Marine Division was pulled out of the line and placed in corps reserve. The 5th and 7th regimental camps were a couple of miles apart. I looked up one day and there was Doug. We had a nice visit that lasted several hours, and he invited me to attend an award ceremony a couple of days later. He was being decorated for the patrol action described previously. Doug was awarded a Bronze Star with a V for Valor, but had he been an officer I believe he would have been awarded at least a Silver Star and perhaps even a Navy Cross. Afterwards I spent some time with him and his squad drinking a few beers. It was pretty apparent that his troops would follow him down the barrel of a cannon. In less than two weeks after the award he was brought up on charges for shooting the prisoners. The case never got beyond the initial hearing and was dismissed as the facts came out.

When our stint in Corps reserve ended the Division redeployed to the main line of resistance. The 1st Regiment moved from corps reserve to division reserve. The 5th and 7th relieved the Army and the Turks on the line. While we were away the Chinese had wrested control of Vegas from the Army. The loss of this outpost caused a lot of resentment toward the Army. A lot of Marine blood had been spilled in March to retain that hill. Beyond the resentment, the loss of Vegas seriously weakened the defensive capabilities of the Marines on outposts Berlin and East Berlin. The 7th Marines barely had time to take off their packs after the relief before the Chinese tried to exploit the loss of Vegas by taking these two outposts. Since they were less than 350 yards from the main line, their loss could easily lead to a breakthrough if the Chinese were in possession of a staging area that close to our trenches. The battle lasted a couple of days, often with both forces occupying parts of the same hill. Finally after hand-to-hand and close combat the Chinese were driven off.

About this time the subject of a prisoner exchange began to be a hot topic at the truce talks in Panmunjom. Doug was selected for movement back to what was to become

"Freedom Village," where he became sergeant of the guard. The next time I saw Doug was at Ascom City just outside of Inchon. We were there to board ship for the homeward journey. Normal procedure here was to keep all transients quarantined. It turned out that the PFC in charge of the keys to the compound at night was an old friend from Camp Le Jeune days. We were his guests at the EM club the nights we spent there. This PFC had 32 months in the Corps at this point and referred to himself as "Almost Corporal" Prall.

As soon as we were settled aboard ship, Doug gave me $450 to hold for him with the express instruction that under no circumstance should I give him that money before we got to San Francisco. He then went off in search of a poker game. He played almost non-stop all the way home, pausing only for a few hours sleep. He missed most of the meals, choosing to subsist on sandwiches and leftovers that I and other guys brought to where he was playing cards. Missing the food probably never harmed him but the chow lines were where the medical staff handed out anti-malaria pills. These pills were to be taken in some formula of so many pills in so many days to be effective.

I knew when Doug gave me the money that it was inevitable that he would come to me at some point and insist I give it to him. When he showed up with the request I told him no, several times in fact. It was his money after all and he was insistent. He was in a game of seven-card stud that was on hold until he returned with more money or to fold his hand. He was sitting on a full house and the only other player in the hand did not have a pair on the board. Very shortly he was back, without the money. The guy betting against him had three eights in the hole to go along with the one up on the board. He brooded for about ten minutes, not about losing the money but for not theorizing what the other guy's hole cards may have been.

Our ship docked at Treasure Island Naval Station. We were given clean dress uniforms and a hundred bucks and told to come back for more money if we needed it. On our visit to San Francisco we went to Kezar Stadium and watched a Forty-Niner game. It rained a little at the game and our wool uniforms didn't smell too good. In an attempt to get a two-for-one we went to a movie thinking the uniforms could dry while we soaked up the picture. The smell was too much and we left in the middle of the film to go to a dry cleaning shop where we had our uniforms pressed and dried all in one swell foop. Now we looked so good it was time to go somewhere nice.

There is a building in San Francisco named the Marine Corps Memorial. We headed over there and on the 8th floor found a very nice cocktail lounge and bar. We grabbed a couple of bar stools and ordered two beers. Doug said he would be right back; he was going to go call his folks and see how things were at home. He had not been gone very long when a master sergeant crawled up on his vacant stool. I explained to him that the seat was taken and the occupant would be back momentarily. He looked at the two stripes on my arm and mumbled some shit about I don't see anyone and sat down in Doug's seat. I then told the good sergeant that the fellow who was sitting there was not going to be happy to find his place had been taken. The master sergeant said, "Fuck him!" Doug looked a little perplexed to find a six striper sitting on his stool and asked if I had told him the seat was being saved. I said I had and Doug asked the master sergeant if he would please move. The response was something like, "Shove off. I ain't movin!" Doug said, "OK, but you won't mind if I take my beer."

With that he reached between me and the master sergeant and picked up his beer bottle and in one swift motion tried to break it on the master sergeant's head. Well, that got him off of Doug's stool but it would have been unwise for us to stay around and use it. The master sergeant was out like a light and spread out on the barroom floor, the bartender was on the phone, and everyone in the room except us wondered what the hell was going on. We weren't in the room much longer. There was a stairwell and we went down those eight flights in a speed that has to be close to a world's record. As we opened the stairwell door leading to the lobby we saw a swarm of MPs getting into the elevator. As soon as the elevator doors closed we left the building. Too bad. It was a nice place with good prices and I would have liked to go back there again sometime.

When our ship pulled into Treasure Island I had only about forty-five days left on my enlistment. All I had was the one uniform they gave us there and I had thirty days leave on the books. Rather than provide me with an entire new issue for two weeks of service, after leave I was processed for immediate discharge. In this case "immediate" took about eight days. Doug had four months of service remaining and he was transferred to the East Coast, Quantico, Virginia, I think. He shipped out a couple of days before my processing was completed and that was the last time I saw him.

Several times in later years I was in New York on business and made several attempts to track him down. The closest I came was the time I reached his sister in New Jersey. She told me he was living in Brooklyn, but was not there at that time. He was at a Veteran's clinic in New England being treated for malaria. Missing the treatments while playing poker had caught up to him. On subsequent trips I tried by starting the search in Brooklyn. These were fruitless and I was never again able to reach his sister either. I concluded that it just was not meant to be for us to ever reestablish contact. In some ways it may have been better for me in the long run because the man was a lightning rod.

What became of Doug remains a mystery to me. What hasn't changed is that he remains in my memory as one of the most unforgettable people I have ever known. He certainly had his share of vices and it takes a real stretch of the imagination to visualize him guarding Heaven's scenes. However, as a friend and fellow Marine, he exemplified the creed. Semper Fi, ole Dougie!

This is my friend Al Baron. Quiet and unassuming—and a hell of a Marine.

Al

Al was a member of the same platoon as I in boot camp. I got to know him better at a later time in Camp Le Jeune. He was a cousin to Del, who was the Assistant BAR man in our fire team. Naturally Del and I became good friends and often when we hit the slop chute Al would come along. Where I really got to know Al was when we were assigned to the same fire team in the staging regiment prior to heading to the Far East. Del exercised an opportunity to transfer to the 8th Marines and so did not see service in Korea. Al and I became pretty close friends and pulled some memorable liberty nights on the West Coast. Upon arriving in Korea, Al was sent to the 1st Marine Regiment and I to the 5th, so we saw each other only occasionally during that time. There are three things that occurred that make Al memorable to me. Two of them occurred in California and the other in Japan.

In writing about Doug I describe an adventure in Tijuana during a liberty we pulled. Al was a member of that quartet. I won't repeat the entire episode here and while it was a night I will always remember, I'm not sure how much recall Al would have of the latter stages of that night. It was Al's hat that I placed in my jacket for safekeeping and forgot I had it when the MPs gave us so much grief.

The second event that I gratefully associate with Al took place in Kyoto, Japan. I was on my first night of R&R in a U.S. Government-run hotel. I had just left the restaurant where I had eaten my first meal off of a plate in about 8 months, the enjoyment of which was slightly tarnished by the presentation. I had ordered fish, never dreaming it would be served Japanese style with the heads and tails still attached. While that was something I was unaccustomed to, the worst part was having the fish's eyes staring at me through the whole eating process. Full and feeling the need for a drink, I moved to the hotel bar and ordered a vodka and tonic.

The bartender had no more than placed my drink in front of me when a Japanese girl sat on the next stool and struck up a conversation. I bought her a drink and while we were talking three soldiers entered the bar and sat at a table just behind our stools. One of the soldiers detached himself and approached the girl and asked her to leave with him. It was obvious that they knew each other prior to the moment. She declined to leave and he became angry and more insistent. She again refused and he and his buddies left.

We had another drink or two and she offered to show me around Kyoto. When we left the building, the aforementioned three soldiers were waiting for us on the sidewalk. He again insisted that she leave with him and she again refused. I'd only met this girl less than an hour ago and wasn't inclined to tackle three soldiers in her defense, particularly since I had no illusions about protecting whatever virtue she had remaining.

It became apparent to me through the conversation that the problem was that this GI was stationed in Kyoto and after a relationship with this young woman wanted her to become exclusively his girl. She on the other hand had no intention of agreeing to such a relationship. I still did not want to get into a brawl with these three dogfaces but the fact that he was a rear echelon pogue and one with a particularly annoying manner was causing the bile to rise in my throat.

Just as I was calculating what his friends response might be if I smeared this guy, a voice from behind me asked, "You got a problem here, Dave?" When I looked over my shoulder there was Al and another Marine I didn't know, but they both looked real good to me right at that moment. The Marines had landed!

With the arrival of the reinforcements the soldiers decided to break off the encounter and left the scene. The other Marine was named Bill, and he was serving with Al in the 1st Regiment. Al and Bill had been in Kyoto for a couple of days before my arrival, but we teamed up for the remainder of their stay. We were never completely drunk during that period but no one would accuse us of being sober, either. I even learned to stare right back at the fish during dinner.

The last occasion I remember sharing with Al was after we got back to California. Having all come home on the same ship, Al, Doug, and I teamed up for a night on the town in San Francisco. Here were three of the four of us who had pulled the last liberty together before going overseas reunited after each serving in a different regiment while overseas. The fourth member of our expedition to Tijuana didn't make the return trip. In his place that night we were joined by another Marine whose name was Stan.

A day or two after this excursion Al and Stan and I were discharged, while Doug was transferred to another duty station. It has been more than fifty years since I last saw any of these guys but they have remained in my memory and my heart along with a large number of other Marines I was privileged to know and serve with. As long as men like these answer our country's call for warriors, we will be secure in the world.

Tom

Tom and I never really became close friends. Not that there was ever a problem between us, but Tom had been in Korea for about 9 months when I arrived. Like a lot of "short timers," Tom had begun to withdraw into himself and limit his exposure.

We came off Hill 229 at the end of December 1952, and Tom immediately began to fret. He had done the calculations and realized he would not be rotated home before the company pulled one more tour on line. For Tom it might be only a partial tour, but in his mind that was even worse.

His situation was not unique, and different guys handled it in different ways. What made Tom memorable were his actions once we returned to the line. The sector we occupied in late January was decidedly more hostile than the ground we covered on 229. It was still winter in Korea, and everyone wore several layers of clothes. About halfway down the reverse slope of our hill there was a head—a 4-holer, sandbagged up to the height of a sitting man. In addition there was a 2 x 4 frame supporting a canvas roof to keep rain and snow from interfering with one's inevitable duty.

This is why Tom is memorable. He made head calls like no one before or since. He would bunker hop until he was at the bunker closest to the head. There he would pause just inside and go into his BM prep. This included undoing his belt, unbuttoning his cold weather trousers, undoing his utility trousers, and being sure his long johns were not entangled in his multiple shirts. Then he would tear off and neatly fold several pads of toilet paper. All this done he would bolt from the bunker, holding up his pants with one hand, toilet paper firmly grasped in the other, and streak to the head. Elapsed time from departure to return was never more than two minutes, usually less. Now that is what I call "potty training."

Tom was rotated home to New England. One can only hope that with his return to civilian life he has been able to develop a more normal and less stressful response to nature's call.

Charlie

Every war or conflict produces a few men who are a different breed from the rest. These men seem to thrive on the chaos that attends combat. Some observers might label such men as psychotics or sociopaths. In all probability the labelers formed these opinions at a safe distance from the hostilities. Further, it's almost a certainty that they never served in combat or personally knew how comforting it was to have men like this on their side of the barbed wire.

I knew such a man. He was a buck sergeant, a squad leader in the machine gun section of Weapons Platoon B Company, 5th Marines. It may be that we, his fellow Marines, all thought he was a little eccentric too, but he was admired and a welcome sight in the trenches. This sergeant's name was Charlie, and by the time I got to the 1st Bn. 5th, he had been with the outfit for over a year and a half. Each month when the roster was made up for the rotation draft back to the States, Charlie would decline rotation and extend his tour in Korea. It was also bandied about that Charlie had turned down promotion to staff sergeant, section leader, more than once. The reason being, so the story went, was that as section leader Charlie would have to spend more time directing squad leaders and less time in the gun pit. I can't officially vouch for the authenticity of the tale, but I believed it then and I believe it today.

Charlie was not content to just let events occur. He directed the KSCs (Korean Service Corps) to prepare signs for him in both the Korean and Chinese languages, which he took into no-man's land and planted on rice paddy dikes. These signs all had an arrow pointing to our lines and captions that read "This way to Charlie's." Because of his long tenure in combat, Charlie also was acknowledged as something of an expert in the siting and construction of bunkers. He was often consulted on the best place to put a bunker so that it would be least likely to be hit by incoming mortar or artillery fire. Most Marines coming on line considered themselves fortunate if they ended up in a bunker that had been sited by Charlie, or one for which he had supervised the construction.

Over his protest, Charlie was finally ordered home. As best as I can recall, he served more than eighteen months in Korea. It may have been some consolation to him that a ceasefire was agreed to shortly after his departure. He stayed in the Corps, and I would wager he was among the first to volunteer for duty in Vietnam.

I seriously doubt that Charlie would remember me, but I will never forget him. I have had a couple of occasions to remember Charlie in the recent past. The first was while watching the movie *Patton* when the general is looking out over a battlefield and says, "I love it! God help me, I love it!" I doubt that Charlie would ever be so dramatic or eloquent, but I am sure he would understand the sentiment. The other more recent reminder was a bumper sticker I saw in a catalog. It read, "Happiness is a Belt Fed Weapon." That was Charlie!

The Great Shit Detail

In Marine Corps parlance any unpleasant assignment is referred to by the troops as a "shit detail."

In January 1953, my battalion (actually it was the colonel's battalion) was in regimental reserve, and the weather was brass monkey cold. Our reserve area was about two miles behind the lines. We were bivouacked in 12-man squad tents which were terraced on the reverse slope of a hill. Each tent had two diesel fueled pot-bellied stoves, one at each end of the tent. Unfortunately, the supply of diesel available would only allow burning the stoves 3 or 4 hours a day. This situation was remedied with typical Marine Corps logic. Since the fuel supply only provided three or four hours of warmth, let's get the troops out of those cold tents the rest of the time.

One of the ways this was accomplished was to hold reveille at 2 a.m. Once we were upright, we were loaded onto trucks and shuttled to the reverse slope of the MLR where we were formed into working parties (shit details), issued equipment, and passed through the lines to repair or add to barbed wire obstacles in front of our lines. This was a shit detail in the truest sense, but only leading up to "The Great Shit Detail."

At the end of the first day of doing this we learned that the signal to secure from the work was when it got light enough for the Chinese to see where we were working. They would usually signal us that visibility had improved by firing a few 76s at us. Their 76s, like our 75s, were a very high velocity, flat trajectory weapon designed for penetrating armor or busting bunkers and not as effective an antipersonnel weapon as a mortar, but we were not going to tell them. The speed of the projectile created a shrill screaming noise as it came in. I never heard a banshee scream but I would wager a 76 would embarrass a banshee in a screaming contest.

Having done this every day for almost two weeks, it was not an activity one looked forward to. I awoke one morning feeling very poorly, so I turned in for sick call. The corpsman gave me some pills and a light duty slip for twenty-four hours. My temperature that morning was just below 102 degrees, and I went back to the sack.

A few hours later, as it began to get light, our first sergeant was making his rounds of the company area. He about shit a brick when he found me in my sleeping bag. Before his walk was over he had found five or six other guys, all with high temperatures and light duty slips. We were all ordered to assemble at his tent where he delivered his well-rehearsed "there will be no goldbricking in his outfit" speech and promptly assigned each of us a detail to perform around the camp.

I drew the job of burning out the shitters. One of the other "malingerers" was tasked to burn out the piss tubes. A piss tube was an empty 155mm casing buried upright in a bed of rocks and lime.

So, off I go to the supply tent to pick up a five-gallon jerry can of gasoline, and armed with my trusty Zippo lighter, head for the nearest four-hole crapper. Being a city boy, I had never done this sort of thing before, but how tough could it be? I poured half the can into one of the holes, peeled off some toilet paper, fired it up and tossed it into the hole. "KABOOM," and it was goodbye shitter. The lid of the four-holer went straight up, taking with it the canvas roof. The canvas walls were covered with pieces of the flaming contents of the pit, as was my field jacket. My eyebrows were gone, too.

As soon as the first sergeant realized we were not under enemy bombardment, he headed in my direction and en route found his voice. He was about midway through his dissertation on how I must be the dumbest S.O.B. in the entire Marine Corps, when "KABOOM," another explosion. Seems I was one of the two dumbest S.O.B's in the Corps. The guy sent to burn out the piss tubes had poured in a healthy dose of gas and then reached in to light it with a match. He had to be evacuated with severe burns to his hand and his face. I felt bad for him, but it did get the first sergeant off my ass. This was the "Great Shit Detail."

A sidelight of this episode is that when the wire laying detail came back that afternoon, the Battalion Medical Staff made the rounds of every tent taking the temperature of every Marine. They were concerned about the possible outbreak of a flu epidemic. Our Company was scheduled for guard duty that night and the guard was made up of the troopers with the lowest temperatures. I stood guard that night with a temperature of over 101 degrees. I only made one more wire laying detail, and then I started to volunteer for clutch platoons, which were sent on line at twilight each evening to reinforce or fill in on the MLR as needed. When we returned to the company area each morning we had the day off and were exempt from shit details, which was a much safer way to make a living in my opinion.

Incidentally, within the past two years I have read a book written by another Marine who was in Korea in the same time frame as me. In that book there is a description of an incident similar to this that happened in his company area. Wish I could let my old first sergeant know about that one.

*Joey and me early in 1953 outside the
main and only entrance to our home
away from home.*

Joey

Most guys named Joseph end up being called Joe. Joey was just not a Joe type. He was a tall, thin kid with skin so white he was only a fart-skin from albino. His blond hair grew in ringlets and over the six or seven months he had been in Korea they had gradually conformed to the contour of his helmet. If it had not been for the camouflage cover on Marine helmets it would have been difficult to tell at a glance whether he was wearing one or not. Barbershops were few and far between. I think the closest professional barber was either in Japan, or maybe San Francisco.

Joey was proud to tell one and all that he was a "Greenpoint Boy." When Joey said it though, it came out "Greenpernt Boy." After a time I became aware that Greenpoint was a neighborhood in Brooklyn and that "The Greenpernt Boys" were supposed to be only slightly less famous than Brooklyn itself. I met Joey when I joined the company on a hill designated as 229. He was one of the guys in the bunker I was assigned to.

I was later to become aware that 229 was the most desirable—that is, the safest—stretch of terrain within the entire 1st Marine Division front. It was the highest ground we held, and the neutral corridor leading to Panmunjom ran across the left flank of the hill. The bunker that I was assigned to was enormous by frontline standards, housing eight Marines on the reverse slope.

The first incident which I remember about Joey

occurred on 229. It was normal to have a 100% watch during hours of darkness. This was reduced to either 50 or 25% during daylight hours. Coming off an all night watch, troops pretty much did what they thought needed doing— eating, cleaning weapons, sleeping, etc. It was Joey's habit to sleep for a while. What made him different from other Marines in this respect was that while most guys just climbed into the sleeping bags without their boots, Joey completely disrobed.

Hill 229 was not only high, it was also steep. November and December are cold months in many places, but in Korea they can be frigid. These are the ingredients. Now visualize eight Marines in a bunker at the top of a high, steep hill that is covered with snow in arctic like temperature. One of these Marines is asleep, nude, in his sleeping bag. Among the other seven are a few looking for a diversion. It was only a matter of time before one of them would say, "I know, let's roll Joey down the hill."

He finally stopped rolling about two thirds of the way to the bottom in about a foot of snow. He unzipped the bag to the point he could tuck it under his armpits, leaving his arms and shoulders exposed, and proceeded to hop up the hill.

After a very laborious climb amid much cheering and hooting, he finally arrived back at the bunker. Not being sure who the culprits were, he reviled one and all. He then took his bayonet from under his cot and climbed back into the bag, and made sure everyone could see that his other hand was on the quick release tab of the sleeping bag. In a matter of minutes Joey was once again fast asleep. There were no bag rollers willing to take the chance that Joey would get the bag open before they could get him out of the bunker. Like the fairy tales say, he slept undisturbed ever after.

A second Joey story has to do with a one-day pass to Seoul. He had been in Korea for nine or ten months by this time and had never had a pass to the rear. It was in late winter and the pass involved a very cold, three-hour ride in the back of a truck. But to Joey, it was worth it for a day in the city. He and the other Marines in the liberty party wore side arms. Well, as Greenpernt Boys are wont to do, Joey and another Marine sought out the company of a couple of ladies of the evening. In this case, I suppose they could be referred to as ladies of the afternoon.

Joey had no more than concluded the terms under which this business was to be conducted when in burst a couple of army MPs. These guys are in starched and pressed uniforms, colored scarves at their throats, and wearing chromed helmet liners and patent leather web gear. That alone would make most Marine infantrymen want to puke, but these GIs didn't know when to quit.

They told Joey they were giving him five minutes to get dressed and clear out. Joey's response was that they wouldn't know whether he was gone in five minutes or not, because he was only giving them two minutes to disappear. With that he un-holstered his .45 pistol and jacked a round into the chamber. The MPs hesitated a second or two trying to decide if this scrawny, pale little jarhead could possibly be serious. They concluded he was and that this was not a matter worth getting shot over, and they were well gone before the two minutes elapsed.

When we returned to the line Joey had only a couple of weeks before his rotation date home came up. He had to weather a few more hairy episodes but finally left with all his body parts in place and in working order. If I have a message for Joey, it is sleep warm, and for Christ's sake get a tan. Glad you made it ok pal.

Marines Retake Peak in Korea

SEOUL, March 27 (*P*)—U. S. Marines tonight regained outpost Vegas from fired-up Chinese Reds. Twenty-four hours earlier the Communists had wiped out all Leathernecks there in a surprise smash.

The Marines recaptured the western front outpost after 10 hours of bitter, costly hand-to-hand trench fighting.

A Marine regimental commander said the Chinese killed or captured every Leatherneck in small holding forces on Vegas and nearby Reno outposts when 3,500 Reds seized the positions in a surprise night attack.

The commander of the 5th Marine Regiment said at 9:45 p. m. tonight (6:45 a. m., Chicago time), his Leathernecks were in firm control of Vegas. They had sent for supplies to dig in and rebuild the shattered outpost.

The 1st Marine Division troops secured the hill at 7:30 p. m., but mopping up operations continued two hours more on the upper slopes.

ROUT 12 COMPANIES

The Marines reported they destroyed the effectiveness of from 12 to 15 Chinese companies—more than 2,000 troops—in bloody fighting. Their commander messaged:

"We are on the top, situation well in hand. Enemy has tried several attempts to reinforce and counter-attack."

Withering Red machine-gun fire had ripped at the Marines on their way up the slope. Marine tanks hammered at the Communist machine-gun nests. Smoke from exploding shells shrouded the outpost.

The Marines smashed through a ring of trenches circling the hill to regain Vegas, after a day of bloody, hand-to-hand combat. Marine searchlights criss-crossed the battlefield to pinpoint Red positions.

The Reds pounded the outpost with mortar and 76 mm. fire, hinting at a possible Chinese counter-attack.

USED MASS FORCE

Before the Marines regained Vegas, Col. L. W. Walt, a Marine regimental commander, said:

"The Chinese took the position by mass force and mass formation, which they can always do on an outpost like that when they want to pay the price.

"We are going to get it back. It's only a matter of when."

The Reds still clung to Reno and to Old Baldy, 2 miles north of Seoul. Old Baldy was captured Wednesday from the U. S. 7th Infantry Division.

126

March 26, 1953

Sometimes it occurs to me that any problems I have with remembering the dates of birthdays, anniversaries, and the like would not exist if all these events could have been arranged to happen on March 26. Each year since 1953 I have been keenly aware of the coming of that day in March.

I remember it as the day when the battle for the outposts Reno, Carson, and Vegas began. It began for me about a half hour before nightfall. I was standing just outside our reverse slope sleeping bunker, smoking a last cigarette before getting ready to go on our standard 100% watch after dark. From where I was standing the hill fell away sharply to a valley about 200 yards in width from north to south where the next interminable row of Korean hills rose up. At the base of the hill there was a supply/tank road that ran east and west, paralleling the MLR. Across the road and in line with our bunker was a helicopter evacuation station for the more seriously wounded. About 150 yards to the east there was a north-south road that came down through a saddle in the row of hills behind us and ended in a T-intersection with the east-west road. On the reverse slope of that next row of hills immediately adjacent to the north-south road was the position of our battalion's 81mm mortars.

As I stood there I was facing sort of to the southeast. Before I could hear the sound, I saw the greasy black cloud of an incoming artillery or mortar round blossom on the forward slope of the hill behind which our 81s were located. I didn't give this a lot of significance at first because it was not unusual for "Luke the Gook" to throw in a round or two now and then and hope to get lucky. This time though, before the distinctive "Kah-Rumph" of an exploding incoming shell reached me, three or four more shell bursts became visible. It was obvious to me now that Luke was firing a search and traverse mission and had some idea where our 81's position was. All in all, I counted nine rounds that landed in three rows of three shells each and formed a boxlike pattern. Fortunately for our team the adjustment after the first three rounds took the pattern down the forward slope toward the valley. Had the second and third rows of the pattern been adjusted to the south, there could have been a lot of damage done. As a mortar man I remember thinking what a nice tight pattern they had fired, and that may have been my last rational thought for four or five days.

Just as I finished my smoke and turned to go in and get my gear the shit really hit the fan. The entire valley below us became one huge impact zone for enemy incoming of all sizes. Simultaneously the forward slope and the crest of our hill became saturated with machine gun and flat trajectory fire of every possible caliber. The fire remained both intense and constant for hours which turned into days. There was nothing to be done except take cover and wait for our big gear to respond. I cannot recall a time in my life, before or since, when I have been so terrified. I'm talking about abject terror here. That's scared shitless times five to the tenth power. God Bless Chet! He's the guy I ended up with in the bottom of a 60mm mortar gun pit. After about an hour of this exploding rain, I said to Chet, "Let's get the fuck outta here!" Chet says, "Great idea! Where do you wanna go?" We stayed where we were. To raise a body part above the level of the sandbags around that pit would have been an instant amputation.

Our gun pit was connected to the command post by a sound power phone network. How it remained intact that night is a marvel. We heard a whistle, which indicated someone was on the line. It was a report from the CP that Charlie Company, on our right flank, was reporting 200 casualties. It occurred to me to ask, "Friendly or enemy?" The answer was friendly! Since a Marine rifle company at that time had a full strength of only a little over 200 men, it kinda puckered your ass while you wondered if anyone was watching the store over there or if we should expect a visit from new neighbors.

Time passed with no apparent let up in the volume of the incoming shells. We were now aware that our artillery had unlimbered and was responding. We could hear the outgoing shells screaming overhead on their way out interspersed with the screams and whistles of the incoming. How these projectiles avoided colliding in midair is a mystery to me because by the sound there was no space to spare. I have no words that would adequately describe the noise level. There were shells traveling in both directions, each having its own sound, with explosions every second or two followed by the whistle and flutter of shrapnel going past. Added to this was a constant hum and buzz of machine guns and other small arms raking the ridgeline without let up. This went on for the entire night of the 26th and into the daylight hours of the 27th when some new but most welcome sounds were added to the din. These were aircraft engines, exploding bombs and 20mm cannon fire. Corsair jockeys were coming in from the south, strafing as they came in on their bombing runs. They were so low that the shell casings ejecting from their wings were falling into our hole and were still hot to the touch.

At some point during the hours of darkness the folks in command finally determined that the Chinese objective in all this was to capture the three outposts in front of Charlie Company, 5th Marines. These three hills were called Reno, Carson, and Vegas. The risk factor associated with the namesake cities was not a coincidence. In rough numbers there were approximately 40 Marines on each of these hills, so the combined total on all three was less than 150 men.

After several probes all along the MLR to confuse and mislead the defenders, the Chinese finally launched an attack of 3500 men against the three Marine outposts. The sheer size of the attacking force and the simultaneous assault on all three hills precluded them from supporting each other.

Carson, which was closest to our main line at 800 yards, was able to draw fire support from the MLR and prevent the Chinese from surrounding them. The Marines there beat off several assaults of numerically superior Chinese formations and Carson remained in our hands.

The other two outposts were further from the MLR. Vegas was about 1300 yards out and Reno was 1800 yards from the nearest help. The Chinese held several hills closer to these outposts than we were. During the earlier hours of this battle, we were kept busy firing missions in support of Carson and in front of our own company where there was some activity reported. I think everyone was hoping the gooks would mass for an infantry assault on our lines because then they would have to lift their barrage. Around 10 p.m. airplanes arrived on the scene and began flying the battlefield from east to west and back again while kicking out a flare every so often. After that it did not get dark again for a couple of days because for the next couple of nights the flare planes were on the scene at twilight.

Shortly after the first flare plane arrived our forward observers were able to find targets. The enemy in company size units could clearly be seen streaming thru the valleys on their way to reinforce and consolidate their gains. One of the FOs told me that it was like kicking the top off an anthill. The ones on their way to Reno and Vegas were beyond the maximum range of our 60mm mortar, using the ammunition as it came out of the containers. While Chet and I manned the gun, we had four ammo bearers in the ammo bunker breaking out rounds and adding a fifth charge to the fin assembly. The rounds came with four and firing with four charges and the tube at a 45-degree angle we could hit targets at a range of over 1900 yards. We didn't know

Marines Avenge Buddies

SEOUL, March 27 (INS)—Counter-punching American Marines recaptured Vegas Hill tonight. The fight to avenge their buddies, killed there yesterday, climaxed nearly 24 hours of seesaw battling. The capture followed ferocious man-to-man combat in Vegas' trenches.

SEOUL, March 27 (AP)—U. S. Marines and Chinese Reds were locked in savage battle today for Vegas outpost, captured by 3,500 Communists.

U. S. 1st Marine Division troops, fighting hand-to-hand, battered their way into the lower trench line of the smoking height, while other Leathernecks charged toward the top.

Col. L. W. Walt, Ft. Collins, Col., a Marine regimental commander, said every Leatherneck on Vegas and Reno when the Reds first hit is presumed either dead or taken prisoner.

The number, of course, was withheld. Walt added:

"The Chinese took the position by mass force and mass formation which they can always do on an outpost like that when they want to pay the price. We are going to get it back. It's only a matter of when."

The Marine assault was supported by thundering rocket and tank fire. The hill was shrouded with smoke from exploding shells, reducing visibility to a few yards.

More on Page 27

2d Time

Marines Back on Key Outpost

SEOUL, March 28 (AP)—U. S. Marines captured outpost Vegas again today in a bitter hour of fighting up its slopes.

Rooting Chinese from trenches, they slammed back a Red counter-attack at the crest and won back the low western front hill for the second time in two days.

Vegas fell Thursday night under a Red attack Monday night, when 3,500 Chinese swarmed around Old Baldy, 26 miles northeast. The Reds still hold Baldy, a target for Allied artillery and bombs.

As ground fighting roared on, American Sabrejets clashed with MIGs over North Korea, knocking down one and damaging four others, the Air Force said.

The kill established the war's 29th jet ace—Col. James K. Johnson, of Phoenix, Ariz.

Johnson, commander of the 4th Fighter-Interceptor Wing, now has 5½ MIGs destroyed, three probably downed and seven damaged.

Marines Again Fight To Hilltop

SEOUL, Korea — (UP) — Battle-weary American marines in their bloodiest fighting in six months won the top of battered Vegas Hill Saturday for the second time in 10 hours.

The exhausted leathernecks then beat off a desperate Red counter-attack.

"The Marines are in complete control of the top. Our purpose is to stay there," an American commander said.

* * *

IN THE AIR, Allied Sabre jets shot down one Communist MIG-15 and damaged three others in battles with the Russian - built planes over northwest Korea.

The Marines took vital Vegas Hill near Old Baldy Mountain from the Chinese after 30 hours of continuous fighting.

It was the fourth time in 36 hours the hill had changed hands.

where the fifth charge would take the rounds but we knew the Chinese were outside our max range with four charges. We fired a nine round search and traverse and the FO reported back that we were right on target and should keep firing search and traverse missions on the same azimuth. The purpose was to kill Chinese, but if they could not use the corridor where our shells were landing we would at least keep them from reaching Reno and Vegas. I worked the traversing hand wheel, kept the tube at forty-five degrees oriented to Reno, leveled the bubbles between shots, and gave the command to fire. Chet dropped the rounds into the tube and swabbed out the barrel every so often.

We fired this mission for a couple of hours and then sometime in the wee hours of the morning several things went wrong within seconds of each other. The night firing device that illuminated the sight and allowed me to check the elevation and bubbles went dead. This happened just as I was struggling to maintain an angle on the tube that would put the rounds into the target zone but also clear the crest of the hill we were firing from. What had been happening gradually as we fired with five charges was that the increased recoil was causing the base plate to sink into the ground. This continually changed the relationship of the tube and the bipod to the base plate, making it ever more difficult to be sure we were going to clear our hill.

I had no choice but to call the CP and report the gun out of action, knowing full well what the response was going to be. I was right on the money, too. The orders were repair the night firing device and reset the base plate and get back into action. During all this time there had been no discernable let up in the rate of incoming fire. The gooks must have been stockpiling ammo for months to sustain that rate of fire. I guess that's why they bothered with the truce talks because it gave them opportunities to do stuff like that.

Being a rational person, and one who was scared shitless to boot, I took a very logical approach to the order just issued. It made no sense to me to reset the base plate if

I couldn't see the sight on the mortar. Resetting the base plate might involve all of us having to leave the gun pit to collect rocks upon which to reset the plate. So while logical but not too rational we took the night firing device into the ammo bunker, which was covered so we could work on it there—not too rational because in order to see what we were doing we had to light a candle. A candle in an ammo bunker? Hell, it was a lot safer than leaving that hole in the ground. The sandbags around our gun pit had more metal in them than they did dirt. While I was working to get the device to illuminate I had the ammo humpers use their helmets to scrape as much dirt as possible from the floor of the ammo bunker and fill several sand bags half full. Against my better judgment and definitely not in my best interest, I somehow got the goddamned firing device to light up. Now Chet and I crawled back out into the gun pit, dug out the base plate, and salvaged any rocks that had not been pulverized by the recoil. By using the sandbags the ammo guys had filled and placing the salvaged rocks on top we were able to get things close enough to level to reset the gun. The twelve or fourteen concentrations we had pre-registered could no longer be fired with any certainty of accuracy and most of our fire would require adjustment by an observer to get on target.

Our first fire mission after I reported the gun back in action was to fire illumination to our company front. Illumination rounds burst in the air and so range was not as critical as elevation. However, I never knew a mortar man who liked firing illumination ammo. The very act of firing these shells ignites a powder train fuse that ultimately sets off the flare itself. The burning powder train creates an arc of burning sparks in the night sky that leads directly back to the muzzle of the firing tube. Over the course of the next three days we spent somewhere around twenty hours a day in the gun pit either firing missions, resetting the base plate, reregistering concentrations, or restocking ammunition supplies. One thing of interest that occurred in one of the other gun pits during this period was a casualty we had in a most unusual way. One of the assistant gunners was dropping rounds into the tube with both hands. It seems he got the round in his left hand over the tube just as the previous round was exiting. The round on its way to Goonieland collided only slightly with the round being held in his left hand. Enough so, however, to drive the round deeper into his hand and the fin assembly severely lacerated his palm. To his credit he stayed on the job until there was enough of a break to get a dressing on it.

The real fight during this time was taking place on Vegas. The decision had been made not to try to retake Reno, and Carson had been reinforced and was holding, but both sides wanted Vegas. I suppose to keep us from applying too many resources in the recovery attempt, the Chinese used their limitless supply of humanity to bring pressure to bear at many different points along the front. They got pretty close to our company front one evening. I remember the casual manner in which the Gunny came into the hootch and after asking if everyone was OK and ready to go on 100% alert, he said he and the skipper thought it would be a good idea if we fixed bayonets tonight. Gulp! The gooks did come calling but were stopped at the wire.

Other than the troops who were on the outposts at the time of the assault, it was the guys who were in reserve who bore the brunt of the recovery of Vegas. The 2nd Battalion 5th Marines was in regimental reserve and the first units called forth were supplied by them. As the battle grew and the Chinks kept reinforcing, it was necessary to bring forward units from the 7th Marines who were in division reserve. The second, third, and fourth days were all too similar to the 26th, and in some ways worse. The noise levels were still painfully high, the incoming was still well above usual levels if not constant, and the aid stations were overflowing with wounded Marines.

I have done a lot of reading from a variety of sources on this battle. Some historians compare this battle to WWII's Battle of the Bulge, and some rate it as even harder fought. For the first twenty minutes of the attack artillery fell on the Marine positions at the rate of one round per second. After that it fell at a rate of a round every forty seconds. The number of Marines killed and wounded over the four days of this battle was very close to 1000. This may have been thought to be the last major battle the Marines would fight in Korea, but on the very day the ceasefire was signed the 1ˢᵗ Marines were engaged in a battle similar to this on outposts Berlin and East Berlin at the eastern-most point on the Marine MLR. Berlin and East Berlin were only about 325 yards in front of the main positions and so could be well-supported in comparison to Reno and Vegas.

This experience was a defining moment in my life. I would be proud to report to you that I acted heroically and played a major role in the defense of our positions. The truth is I am still a little ashamed for being as fear struck as I was. I do take a small measure of pride in having been able respond to orders and not letting my comrades down, but I can't brag about that. I had just turned twenty-one a week and a half before the shit hit the fan, and I had serious doubts about ever being able to legally buy a beer in the USA. Many times since, when life has not been as easy as I would have liked it to be or if there was a situation at work that seemed insurmountable, I have remembered how I felt in late March of 1953, and all of a sudden things weren't nearly as bad as I had let my imagination lead me to believe. I claim no personal credit in this opinion, but I really think the Chinese just fucked with the wrong group of guys and got their asses kicked.

Talk of Truce Brings Lull to Ko

Marines rest in the Vegas Hill area, Korea, as an uneasy quiet comes to the battlefront. The quiet results from a possibility that truce talks will be reopened.

Me and the squad, troopin' & stompin'
Corps Reserve, Camp Casey, May/June 1953

Reserve

Reserve refers to the time when combat units are taken off the line and sent to a rear area. It does not automatically follow that reserve was always a good thing. There were different kinds of reserve, some better than others. None of them are to be confused with R&R (Rest & Relaxation). Marine Corps organization in the 1950s called for all units to be subdivided into components of three. For example:

> 3 regiments to a division
> 3 battalions to a regiment
> 3 companies to a battalion, etc.

The most common tactical arrangement was two-up and one-back, the one back being the reserve component. In this manner the division would have two regiments on line and one regiment in division reserve. Each of the forward regiments would deploy two battalions on line and have the third in regimental reserve. The forward battalions would have all three rifle companies on the line.

From best to worst, the pros and cons of the different kinds of reserve are as follows:

CORPS RESERVE: During the Korean Conflict the 1st Marine Division was in corps reserve one time. All three rifle regiments came out of the line at the same time (Marine tanks and artillery units remained to support the Army divisions and the Turkish Brigade, which replaced the Marines). We were settled into three regimental compounds about twenty miles behind the front. Duties in corps reserve were not dissimilar to stateside routine. We had inspections, training exercises, and lots of things troops coming out of combat considered "chickenshit." However, we ate well and slept comfortably knowing that we were unlikely to be roused in the wee hours to respond to some crisis on the line. The division returned to the lines at the end of June, 1953, just in time for another round of heavy actions that lasted right up to the day the ceasefire took effect.

DIVISION RESERVE: Here an entire regiment would move back to a camp or camps five or ten miles behind the MLR. When the regiment was in reserve it was not normally tasked with duties in support of the troops on the line. Remember that word "normally." The time in the rear was devoted to rebuilding units and restoring the level of training that all Marines are expected to maintain. I recall that during the time the 5th Marines were in division reserve, they loaded us aboard ships and we conducted amphibious landing exercises on coastal islands.

In rare instances, things become other than normal. In late March of 1953, the 1st and 5th Regiments were on line and the 7th Marines were in division rReserve. In the 5th Regimental Sector the 1st and 3rd Battalions were on line and the 2nd Battalion was in Regimental Reserve. Between the 26th of March and April 1st, the 2nd Battalion of the 5th Marines and all three Battalions of the 7th Marines were called up and fed into the lines to plug breaches and counterattack-overrun outposts. As mentioned before, reserve is not automatically a good deal.

REGIMENTAL RESERVE: This was the least desirable of the reserve periods. The major advantage was that units in reserve did not participate in patrols. Regimental reserve was a step in the two-up/one-back scheme of things. The three battalions in the regiment would rotate in and out of line. We would move back to tents about two or three miles behind the MLR, but the living was not as good as in other types of reserve. There was less chickenshit, but in truth most troops would have preferred to stay on the line. Days were spent replacing damaged or lost gear, filling the ranks with replacements, getting a shower and clean clothes. There was also an effort made to reintroduce us to military protocol and discipline. The downside to regimental reserve were the "clutch platoons" and the working details.

Clutch platoons were a group of Marines from the reserve unit who would be sent up to the MLR, usually at dusk, to spend the night. The reasons were varied. The unit on line might be sending out a large patrol and the MLR needed reinforcing while they were out front. At times intelligence believed a certain section of the line was going to be probed that night and they wanted extra men in the trenches. What made this undesirable was that each night you would be in a new place, not familiar with the terrain and not surrounded by your own company mates. Many guys volunteered for the clutch platoons because they found it preferable to the work details. After a couple of weeks of details I, too, volunteered.

The detail I remember as the most distasteful, toilsome, and hazardous was laying wire. We would be awakened at 2 a.m. It was so cold in the tent that an icicle hung from the ceiling of the tent to just short of your face where your breath had frozen during your sleep. We were then trucked to the reverse slope of the MLR and crossed the ridgeline to the forward slope where we advanced in front of our trench line and either repaired artillery-damaged wire or installed additional wire in natural terrain approaches. Laying barbed wire is not a silent activity and our presence was duly noted. The signal to cease work and return to the trucks was when Luke fired the first round—kinda like a starter's gun to begin a race. We did this every morning for about two weeks, and that's when I began signing up for the clutch platoons.

I remember losing a rifle on one of these wire details. I had hung it on a stake to free both hands to work the wire. At first light Luke sent in a couple of 76s that landed between me and my rifle. I didn't wait to see if he was going to make a sight correction; I shagged ass up the hill and dove into the trench line. The captain was pretty pissed that I would leave my rifle in no-man's land and was on the verge of ordering me out to get it. My platoon leader intervened and talked him out of that. A patrol brought the rifle in that night. The stock was blown in two and the receiver and barrel were damaged enough to render it unserviceable.

We were all glad to get back on the hill where we had bunkers for cover, surrounded by friends and somebody else pulling all the shit details.

Pop

There are many sad stories to be told about the troubles that can befall career servicemen. Many can be attributed to failed marriages caused by the long separations which servicemen often endure. In other cases the marriages may have been poorly made to begin with. And, along with and perhaps contributing to the domestic strife, alcoholism is a frequent factor in many of these cases.

If you were in the Corps and half way alert, you would sooner or later see the wreckage of the situations described above. Most, though not all, of these men were good Marines and remained dedicated to the Corps, despite the Corps' lack of appreciation for their individual circumstances or situations. For many of them, when their personal lives disintegrated around them, the Corps was all they had left. Pop was one of these men.

Pop joined us on the MLR early in March of 1953. It was apparent at first glance that he was not your average PFC. Without knowing for certain his actual age, he was obviously in his 30s and quite possibly older. He was a large man with graying hair, and his manner indicated that he was not overwhelmed to be in a combat zone. Despite the age differential, there was never a hint of resentment about taking orders from noncoms barely out of their teens.

As we became better acquainted, Pop shared a little of his history with me. When he joined our unit he had almost thirteen years in the Corps. We all knew he had been around for a while just by his serial number, since it had only six digits. In an outfit like the Corps where seniority is a virtue, six digits almost rated a salute. Marines of my era all had serial numbers of seven digits and I was considered something of an old salt because my service number began with 11.

Pop had been a Marine since 1941 and had been involved in several of the battles as the Marines worked their way across the Pacific toward Japan. He had been wounded twice in different campaigns and was the holder of both the Bronze Star and the Silver Star. He told me that the highest rank he had attained was master sergeant, but he would not discuss the circumstances that led to his reduction in rank.

A story he told me about World War II has stayed in my mind over the years. I don't recall which island he was describing, but Pop talked about coming ashore in a hail of small arms fire from the Japanese defenders. As they moved forward to get off the beach, the fire became even more intense and the cover became even sparser. He spotted a small depression in the earth and gratefully dove in. It took a moment for him to realize that the depression had been made during the pre-invasion naval bombardment. He then realized that he was sharing the depression with an unexploded 16-inch projectile barely covered by a layer of sand. Rather than take a chance on a nearby explosion detonating the shell, he decided he would be better off taking his chances with the small arms fire and sought new cover.

Pop was something of a hard charger. There was a division policy in effect that replacements had to be on the line a minimum of five days before they were allowed in front of our barbed wire. As I recall the purpose was to give the new men a chance to become familiar with the terrain in front of us and to learn the routine of life on the line. Pop chafed under these restrictions. On the ridgeline just forward of our living bunkers was an abandoned observation post. It was small, and would accommodate no more than two prone men. It had a very wide aperture facing the Chinese hills. Since it had been abandoned, the feeder trench that provided access had fallen into disrepair and was less than three feet deep. It provided cover only if a person crawled in on all fours. When Pop learned of the bunker's existence, nothing would do but for him to go have a look. He grabbed a pair of binoculars and headed for the forward slope. He either didn't get low enough or the binoculars reflected some light because he wasn't there two minutes when Luke sent him a "welcome to Korea" greeting. They fired a couple of 76s directly at the bunker to chase him out, and then peppered the route back to the reverse slope with 82mm mortars. Pop looked a little bedraggled when it was all over but he was unscathed. It was just after this adventure that he told me about sharing a hole with the 16-inch shell. Pop's popularity suffered for a day or two because some of the 82s were very close to some of the living bunkers. Proper etiquette on line was not to draw fire when it could be avoided.

I left Korea in December 1953 and Pop was still there. Three years later I reenlisted in the Corps and did five more years before receiving my discharge in February, 1962. I had resumed an interrupted apprenticeship and my wife, our child, and I were living on the South Side of Chicago. Early one morning the phone rang at approximately 5:30 a.m. It was Pop. He apologized for calling so early but was really getting nervous about his surroundings. He was in an all night Bar-B-Q joint in one of the worst neighborhoods in Chicago. He was still in the Corps and explained that he was on his way to Camp Pendleton in California. He was hitchhiking across the country, dead broke, and had no idea where he was in Chicago. He was sure that he wanted to get out of the Bar-B-Q joint, though. I told him I would be there in less than half an hour and for him to be at the curb outside for a fast pick up.

The first thing I noticed as I pulled into the curb was that Pop had remade corporal. I invited him home for breakfast but he declined, saying his time to get to California was fast dwindling. I gave him forty dollars, which was all I could spare, and drove him to Chicago's city limits and left him along side of Route 66 West.

I don't know if he got to California on time or if he ever made sergeant again. I hope he did in both cases and that he eventually was able to retire and take life a little easier. Pop deserved it.

Rosie

Reading the preceding vignettes having to do with guys I knew, one might draw the conclusion that I never met a Marine I didn't like. Believe me, I did, and in the case of Rosie it still pains me to refer to him as a Marine.

Usually when people who do not get along are thrown together by circumstance, they find a way to either ignore one another or settle their differences somehow. In every case except Rosie's, I always felt that regardless of the personal relationship between myself and another Marine, he would still cover my back and I would cover his. I never had this feeling about Roosevelt—that being Rosie's given name.

Actually, I'm the only one who called him Rosie, and I did it solely because I knew it aggravated him. Believe me, it wasn't easy to aggravate him because he was too stupid to recognize an insult most of the time.

The first time I saw him was in the squad tent in early 1953. The squad had been awakened at 2 a.m. to go out and lay barbed wire. It was an absolutely frigid day with steady winds in the 20-25 mile per hour range. When the sun rose that morning the Chinese let us know they didn't want any more wire laid where we were working and, as was customary, drove us off the hill with a barrage of 76mm shells. A couple of guys were hit this day, none seriously and none from our squad, but it does tend to put one in a bad frame of mind. We were looking forward to getting back to the tent and firing up the oil stove and thawing out.

While we were out on the hill that morning the company received replacement drafts, one of whom was Roosevelt. The first thing that struck me was his initial appearance. He had a very poor complexion, but that wasn't his fault. Those of us who had just returned from the wire detail hadn't had a bath or worn clean clothes in at least two weeks and we had been crawling around on our bellies within the last two hours dodging 76s. Compared to Roosevelt, we were ready to stand inspection by the Commandant.

This guy looked just like he had stepped off the lift bringing him up out of the coal mine at the end of a long shift. I was to find out later that in fact he *had* been a coal miner in civilian life, but I didn't know that then. I guess what really got him off on the wrong foot with me and a few others was that the amount of oil per tent was rationed each day and Rosie had burned up over half of our daily allotment, which meant we would all be sitting around in our sleeping bags before dark.

I began to have small problems with him almost immediately. As senior man in the tent, there were things that I was expected to have done daily. Most of them had to do with the welfare of the squad, like getting fresh water and rations brought in and trash carried away. It was never that he would refuse the assignments but it was always necessary to repeat the orders in stronger terms before he would get off his dead ass.

Within a week or ten days after the replacements came in we got orders to saddle up—we were going back on line. We took over a section of the line between A Company on our left and C Company on our right. Our company front was longer than A or C Company's, but they had outposts to man and we did not.

It was really a poor piece of real estate. The Chinese hills in front of us were higher than ours, and there were gaps in our line where there was no hill at all. In order to use the service road that ran parallel to and behind our lines it was necessary to lay smoke to obscure the enemy's vision.

Sometimes after the smoke was laid the trucks would pull right to the base of the last hill and rev their engines without moving forward just to confuse the enemy and draw fire where there was no target. At night these draws were covered by tanks, pre-registered artillery concentrations and, as the situation demanded, a platoon or company from reserve units spending the night in a blocking position on the next row of hills. There was a helipad in the valley just below and behind our platoon positions for evacuating casualties.

The first thing I made sure of when taking over the squad area on line was that Rosie was not in the same bunker as me. He was in a four-man bunker, not enough yards away, but at least there was a degree of relief from him.

We had been on line just a few days. I was on phone watch in the command post when a call came in from the platoon on our left. The platoon leader, a lieutenant who had reported to the company at the same time as Roosevelt, had been seriously wounded by an incoming mortar round. He was on a litter and being shuttled along the trench line to the helipad for evacuation. The request was for our platoon to meet the litter and relieve the bearers.

The lieutenant was a large man and even if he had not been, carrying a litter at top speed in that terrain while being shot at is strenuous work. I left the phone long enough to run to the next bunker, where I found four Marines. I described the situation and told them to get to the juncture of the platoon boundaries as fast as possible. One of the men in the bunker was Rosie.

The other three were immediately out the hatch donning helmets and flak jackets as they went. Roosevelt remained kneeling in the center of the bunker, his attention fixed on a canteen cup and a Coleman stove. I said, "Did you hear me?" His response was that his cocoa was almost ready and he'd be with me in a minute. With that I kicked over the stove, spattering him with the hot cocoa. Before he knew what was coming I grabbed him by the hair, dragged him from the bunker and shoved him up the trail. I may have said something like, "If you don't come back on the end of the litter, they will damn sure take you out of here on one."

They made the swap with the bearers from the other platoon and got to the helipad just as the chopper was weaving in behind what cover our low hills afforded. The lieutenant was taken direct to one of the hospital ships (they had names like "Consolation" and "Repose") that were anchored in Inchon's harbor. We heard later that the he didn't make it.

Later that same day when I was relieved from phone watch my buddy Joey and I decided to add to the sandbags around the entrance and to the roof of our bunker. I had just put down my entrenching tool and was handing sandbags up to Joey when up comes Rosie whining about how I treated him that morning. I never said a word. I just smacked him right in the teeth, sending him on his ass about ten yards down the hill.

While he was getting up I turned and picked up my entrenching tool and I am sure I had it in my mind to finish this asshole once and for all. Joey and two or three other squad members interceded. Had they not, I might very well be writing this from a Naval prison.

There is absolutely no doubt in my mind that we would have clashed again had circumstance not precluded it. Rosie turned into the aid station just a few days later. He complained of a sore throat. Doc, our corpsman, couldn't make a diagnosis so he sent him back to "Easy Med," which was a unit like you would see on an episode of *M*A*S*H*. The doctors there were either not sure what he had or realized it was beyond their ability to treat, so he was evacuated to Japan. I can't say what happened to him from that point because I don't know and didn't care enough to take the time to find out.

I have mixed emotions to this day about that creep. I was glad to be rid of him but I resent that he got out before the Chinese came calling a few days after he left. If my opinion of him is correct I could visualize him back in the States telling everyone how he had to be evacuated from the front lines in Korea. It's been fifty plus years since I last saw this shitbird and I still regret that I didn't get to him with the entrenching tool.

Me and Mikey-San

Mikey-San (Ee Mon Soo)

I'm really not sure why I am making a record of this. It's a foregone conclusion that if my wife or daughters ever read this they are not going to like the facts of the case. I'm not too thrilled with the way the record ends either, but it's long been history and there is no changing things now.

As best any of us in the squad could make out from his pronunciation of his Korean name, it was "Ee Mon Soo", and he was eight or nine years old. He was a skinny little cuss with a lot of teeth showing when he smiled, and he looked even smaller dressed in hand-me-down adult-sized Marine utilities. We were never sure about whether he had family or what had become of them. None of us were comfortable with calling him Ee Mon Soo, so he became "Mikey-San" around the tent.

We first saw Mikey-San when a squad member named Dupree brought him back to the tent. Dupree was a Cajun character from Loozeeanna, and I think we were all a bit surprised at the sentiment he showed when interacting with this small Korean boy. There was a policy in place against fraternization with indigenous personnel, but it was only laxly enforced with respect to little kids. A lot of the tents back in this particular reserve camp had small boys doing chores. This gave the kids some income and provided them with food.

As senior man in the tent, I told Dupe that the boy could stay until someone with more authority than I said he had to go. For his part, Mikey-San had special names for the guys in the tent. When he was pleased with me, I was "Numma One Sahgee-San," even though I was not a sergeant at the time. When he was unhappy with me I was "Numma Hocken Ten." He was not allowed in the mess area, so we each saved part of our meals and brought them back to the tent for him. In turn he did the things he was capable of around the tent. Laundry (washy-washy) and general clean up were things he did well. Other jobs that required more strength he couldn't do, such as hauling a 5-gallon jerry can of water or fuel oil up the slope to the tent.

As the time passed it was evident that the bond between Dupree and Ee Mon Soo was becoming stronger every day. One morning Dupe approached and asked me what I thought his chances were of taking the boy home with him. This was taking place in mid-to-late June 1953, and Dupree wasn't going to have enough time in Korea to rotate home until early 1954. Besides that, our time in reserve was fast diminishing and we would be going back on the line in a week or two, certainly no place where we would take a small boy, even if it were legal. Having no knowledge of what this might entail and no authority to set things in motion I suggested that he either talk to the battalion chaplain or our company commander. He elected to speak with our captain first, who while sympathetic was not too optimistic and tried to bring realization of the difficulty of this request to Dupree. He did send him to see the chaplain.

What the chaplain suggested was that Dupree attempt to get Mikey-San into one of the orphanages sponsored by the U.S. and have him remain there until Dupe's time for rotation was closer and he could open negotiations with the Korean authorities to take Ee Mon Soo out of the country. The chaplain also reiterated to Dupe how this could be very difficult as no one knew if there were other relatives alive who might claim custody of the boy. Arrangements were begun to find a place for Mikey-San to sit out the war or at least to wait until Dupree was closer to a going home date.

We moved back into the lines in late June, and were still there when the ceasefire went into effect at the end of July. Mikey of course had been left behind and I really have no idea what became of him after we left the reserve area. The terms of the truce dictated that each side would dismantle existing fortifications, reduce force levels of the armies facing each other, and pull back a specified distance from the positions held at the time of the ceasefire. As fate would have it, two of the three Marine regiments the 1st and the 7th were pulled back south of the Imjin River. Our regiment, the 5th, remained north of the Imjin and took over responsibility for what had been a division sector a few days before. Had our regiment been one of those posted south of the river, it might have been possible for Dupree to begin a new search to relocate Ee Mon Soo. As it was, the 5th remained north of the river for at least the balance of 1953. I rotated home from there in late November and that was the last time I saw Dupree and I never heard what became of Mikey-San.

I hope something good happened for both of them, but I may just be trying to have optimistic thoughts. I told you, you wouldn't like the ending . . .

Me, Joey Reedy, and Art "Fuzz" Golbach

Hedy

On only one other occasion did my fright level approach the height achieved on March 26. While it was for a much briefer period, it was also much more personal in nature and every bit as intense. The circumstances surrounding this incident take a little background set up.

Many of the outpost hills in front of the Marine lines were named after female movie stars of that era. Last names were not used because, us being Marines, we all knew these babes would want to be on a first name basis with us. Hence the outposts named Marilyn, Ava, Dagmar, Hedy, and so on. Despite the allure suggested by the names, none of these hills was a place Marines cared to spend their nights.

Over time, each of these outposts was tested by the Chinese. Some many times, all more than once, and a few of these confrontations became major battles. Outpost Hedy seemed to be one the gooks really had designs on. Hedy was at the east end of a ridge that ran parallel to the MLR at a distance of not more than a couple of hundred yards out in front. At the other end of this ridge was another Marine outpost called "Bunker Hill." Bunker Hill had been a Chinese hill until the Marines took it away in late 1952. I may be wrong, but I believe there was less distance between the Chinese positions and our lines opposite Hedy than at any other point in the Marine sector. When the ceasefire went into effect and both sides had to dismantle fortifications and move back, it was found we were cohabiting with them on Hedy. The goonies lived on the forward slope and we lived on the reverse slope. Prior to the ceasefire this was a very active position with almost nightly contact reported.

To get back to the incident, it occurred late one night, not on Hedy but in the trench-line just behind the outpost. My battalion was in regimental reserve at the time. Because of the enemy's frequent probing, the reserve battalions provided additional troops to man the lines during the hours of darkness. These platoons were usually volunteers and called "clutch platoons." I was a member of a clutch platoon when the incident happened.

To understand the conditions on the night of this event, visualize a Frankenstein movie. The mad doctor is about to infuse life into his creature. The scene shifts to the outside of the castle. The rain is cascading down, the thunder is deafening and the lightning flashes are so intense and frequent it is almost intermittently night and day.

On just such a night a friend named Don and I were in a two-man fighting hole on the MLR just behind Hedy. The rain was causing the trench conditions to deteriorate and we were standing about ankle deep in mud that had the consistency of oatmeal. Our hole was the next-to-last on the left flank of the company sector. To our left was a machine gun position and then the trench-line began a gradual climb to higher ground that eventually became Hill 229. The holes were connected to the command post by a sound powered phone and it was procedure to call in every fifteen minutes to report our status to the squad leader.

Sometime after midnight, just to be sure we weren't having too much fun, the Chinks began to lob in a few mortar rounds from time to time. The first noticeable effect of this other than adding to the flash bang of the thunder and lightning was that our sound power phone went dead. One of the incoming rounds had severed the wire. This eventuated a system of alternating visits up and down the trench to keep the squad leader apprised of our well-being.

Don had just departed on one such trip when I began to chill and decided to slip into the bunker and put my field jacket on under my poncho. I hung my rifle muzzle down on a peg driven into the side of the hole and ducked into the bunker, which in this particular position, unlike most others, was dug into the forward wall of the trench. I was not in there more than a minute and certainly less than two. When I came up out of the bunker and turned to my right to get back to the fighting hole, I found the way blocked by a body. The person was facing away from me and I immediately noticed he was not wearing a helmet and his poncho was not the camouflaged type worn by Marines. His poncho hung down as ponchos do and while I could not see his hands, it was apparent he was carrying something under the poncho.

I placed my hand on his shoulder and half turned him around with the intention of by-passing him and getting back to the hole. As he turned at the touch of my hand, the lightning lit up the trench and I found myself looking directly into an oriental face. Worse, the lightning flash revealed to me that he was the last in a line of five or six, all dressed just like him and all between me and my rifle. Of course now I was sure that what he had under the poncho was a burp gun. I knew if I turned to run I would be shot in the back so I decided I would at least try to get to my weapon. As I passed one slant-eyed face after another all I could think of was "holy shit" and wonder why they hadn't yet shot me. Meanwhile the thunder and lightning continued with no let up. I think I would rather have met Frankenstein in the trench. If you want to imagine my thoughts and feelings at this moment you will have to recall—and I'm sure it has happened to everyone—how when you are dreaming and the bogey man appears and you can't run and you can't scream! Only in a dream you can wake up.

I was finally able to work my way to the fighting hole only to find a person up on the firing step looking out over no-man's land. I was within an arm's length of my rifle now and I was able to see that the guy on the firing step was wearing a camouflage helmet cover and a poncho just like mine. Hooray! A Marine.

I stepped up next to him and when he noticed me he explained that a machine gun emplacement to our left had collapsed due to a very near miss by one of the mortar rounds after the rain had already weakened the trench. He was setting in the tripod to place the gun in our hole for the night. The Asians in the trench-line were Korean Service Corps workers who were assigned to him to bring over the gun and a supply of ammo. Not too much more time had elapsed when Don returned from checking in. I didn't tell him too much about what had happened while he was gone. He and I were sent down the trench to begin cleaning up the collapsed MG emplacement and continuing our watch from there.

I have tried to make light of this episode in the retelling but let me assure you I was nothing but panic-stricken at the time. It may be just as well that I was not in possession of my rifle when I came out of the bunker. I very well may have shot several of the Koreans who it turned out were on our side. Several months later while I was in NCO school I shared a tent with a corporal who had done just that. He was armed with a pistol and while traversing a dark trench ran into two Asians. He shot and killed both of them and learned after the fact that they were KSC workers. So, on the night I've just described, it would be fair to say the KSCs were lucky I was not armed. It would be even fairer to say that I was even luckier that they were KSCs and not Chinese. I still have vivid memories of the scene and particularly so during violent thunderstorms or when I see an old Frankenstein movie on TV.

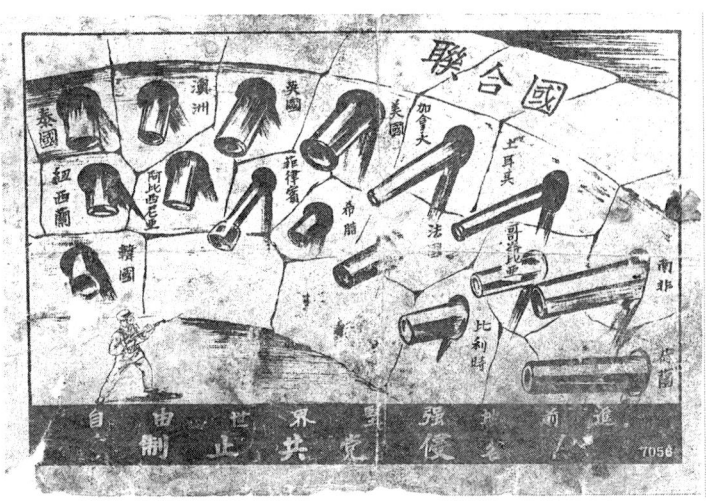

Propaganda leaflet (above) and "Safe Conduct Pass"

161

Lennie on the Kansas Line after the cease fire went into effect.

Lennie and the Poster Girl

The "Poster Girl" was a young woman—almost said young "lady"—that I met while home on leave in the late summer of 1952. The meeting came about in a rather unusual fashion. In my neighborhood in Chicago there was an Eagles Lodge. The building was divided into a barroom, a card room and a huge rental hall. This particular evening I was in the card room deeply immersed in a poker game. That same evening there was a wedding reception in the hall. Late that night when the reception was beginning to break up, this young woman strolled into the card room and began to observe the game in progress. A woman in the card room was a novelty in itself, but this became even more unusual when she asked if she could sit-in at an empty chair. There were no strenuous objections, so she was dealt in.

As the game progressed there was even more cause for raised eyebrows when she lit up a crooked little black Italian cigar. But wait, we still hadn't seen it all. When Hank the bartender took drink orders for the table, we learned that her drink of choice was straight shots of whiskey. This was not your average 18- to 20-year old girl. I don't recall who won or lost in the poker game but when it ended she and I had a couple of more drinks at the bar. I saw her two or three times more before I had to report to California, for, as my orders stated, "Duty beyond the seas."

After arriving in Korea, I was quite surprised to receive a letter from her. She had called my parents to get the

163

address. Enclosed in the letter was a picture of her with a fur draped around her bare shoulders and showing considerable cleavage. If I didn't know she was a cigar smoking, whiskey drinking type, I would have said she looked pretty good. At the time I received the letter we were occupying a bunker that was virtually overrun with rats, and with typical sick Marine humor, I nailed the picture to a board and placed it in front of the main access for our furry little bunker mates. It remained there for a couple of weeks at least and then along came Leonard.

Lennie was a replacement. He was kind of an adolescent kid from the Detroit area who apparently had no girlfriend at home. In any case, once he spotted our rodent control device he began to ask all sorts of questions about the girl in the picture. Eventually he asked me if I would have any objection if he wrote her a letter. Her address was on the reverse side of the picture and I assured him I had only two concerns: he was not to mention me or to tell her what the picture was being used for. The whole thing should have ended there and would have been completely forgettable except for the incident that followed.

It was several weeks later when the gunny stuck his head into our bunker and told me to get my ass up to the company CP, the captain wanted to see me, RIGHT NOW! I could tell by the gunny's tone of voice that I was probably in some kind of a jam but I couldn't think of anything I had or hadn't done that would come to the skipper's attention. I reported in, in the best Marine fashion, and almost before I finished the captain began waving a sheaf of papers in my face and asking me what kind of stupid son of a bitch I was. The papers turned out to be a letter from Headquarters Marine Corps, with endorsements from consecutively less senior officers down thru the chain of command. I pleaded ignorance and it was explained to me that my mother had called the Marine Corps and asked why she had to hear of my being killed in action from an acquaintance of mine rather than being notified through official channels. It seems Leonard had written to this girl and explained that he was writing in my stead because I had been killed in action. She then took the initiative to call my folks and express her condolences and my folks in turn contacted the Marine Corps, who assured her that it was a mistake and I was indeed hale and hearty in the Far East.

This incident led to probably the worst ass chewing I ever endured, but it was small potatoes though compared to the one I gave Lennie back in the bunker. I eventually forgave him and he turned out to be a pretty good hand. I haven't seen Leonard since the end of 1953, and I never saw or spoke to the "Poster Girl" again. End of story!

*Rocky and me enjoying our tour in the
Land of the Morning Calm*

The Rock

No, "the Rock" was not a terrain feature. The Rock, along with Rocky, were nicknames applied to Roscoe. Roscoe was a 27-year old black man from Texas who had been drafted and through chance found himself in the Marine Corps.

Our paths crossed when, again by chance, we were both assigned to the same unit in Korea. In total there were four of us assigned to B Co.1st Bn.5th Marines that day. Rocky and I were in the same platoon but different squads, so while we were never very far apart, neither were we that close most of the time.

Rocky could get downright emotional when explaining how he had been drafted within a month or so of reaching the age of legal exemption from call-up. This of course gained him no sympathy in the company of Marine enlistees. Nevertheless, he remained good-natured despite all the derision sent his way.

The incidents which cemented the Rock in my memories happened later in our Korean tour. There are, though, a few earlier recollections of him in general that I have. He could be brought close to the point of meltdown if we chanced upon Dinah Washington singing "What A Difference A Day Makes" on Armed Forces Radio. We also shared a passion for June Christy, and in particular her rendition of "My Heart Belongs to Only You." Often, in reserve, after a few beers we would get together and sing. As music it was far from great, but as therapy and fun it ranked right up there. I confess though, we did not get a lot of encore requests.

After the ceasefire Rocky and I stood duty together at the main crossing station into Panmunjom and the demilitarized zone. At this site there were observers from a couple of neutral countries, Sweden and Switzerland, I think. There were also some Army MPs there. Because the road ran through the Marine Sector, we were charged with preventing weapons from being taken into the zone and ascertaining that all vehicles and personnel entering had proper authorization. We also had to record vehicle numbers entering and check that they all came out. The only signature we were authorized to accept was that of our regimental commander, a full bird colonel.

During one of the fights before the truce, a Marine tank had been damaged and was left in what became the demilitarized zone. One morning a three-vehicle convoy pulled up to the crossing station. The makeup of the convoy was a jeep, a six-by-six truck with troops in the back, and a tank. I began recording vehicle numbers and collecting personal weapons from the troops and drivers. Rocky approached the jeep to check the authorization. We both recognized the passenger in the jeep as our colonel. Rock asked to see his pass, and the colonel asked Rocky if he knew whom he was addressing. Rocky said, "Yes sir." The colonel then asked if he knew who signed passes authorizing entry. Rock again said "Yes sir. If you sign one for me you can enter." Not very graciously, the colonel filled out and presented Roscoe with a pass. By the time I had finished recording and collecting weapons, Rocky had a pass in hand. He then told the colonel that the jeep and truck could pass, but not the tank. Now the colonel got pissed off. He stated that he needed the tank to tow out the damaged tank. Rock said if they would remove the 90mm cannon and the built-in machine guns, he would allow the tank to pass. After an unsuccessful attempt to bully his way in, the colonel finally ordered the convoy to reclaim their gear and left the scene. The next morning the convoy returned, once again led by our regimental commander. This time he had a pass in hand, and instead of a tank, the third vehicle was a tank retriever, without weaponry of any kind, and no turret. Their passage was routine and a few hours later they returned with the damaged tank in tow.

Our tour at this post extended into the time of the prisoner exchanges. Part of this duty was hard to stomach. We were under orders not to interfere with the passage of vehicles involved in the exchange and had advance notice of their arrival. We could hear the trucks coming, and as they got closer we could also hear the singing and chanting of the Chinese and North Korean prisoners heading for Panmunjom. They were all standing upright and were packed into the trucks like sardines. As they got closer it looked like there were objects blowing out of the back of the trucks. In fact, it was the prisoners throwing away their clothes so that they could claim maltreatment when they arrived at the exchange point. Trucks in the middle and at the end of the convoy were driving over so many jettisoned clothes and shoes that their wheels barely came into contact with the road.

The part that was hard to stomach was the disparity in numbers of, and apparent well being of, the gooks going in and the smaller number of our guys coming out. Not only were they drastically fewer in number, they were all ambulance cases. The numbers are a matter of record but there were over 75,000 of the enemy exchanged. We got back a little over 12,000, mostly South Koreans, but among that total there were about 3600 Americans.

A side light of this event was that the gooks thought that as long as they were going to throw their shoes away, they might as well throw them at their former enemies. We were pretty sure that retaliation of any kind would be frowned upon, so we moved down the road a piece where we were out of sight of the neutral observers and Army MPs. There we built a decent supply of fist-sized rocks. Thereafter, all offerings of shoes were met with a rock in return. It was of little concern to either of us that the shoe launcher had sped down the road before we could react. They were all gooks, and a truckload was hard to miss at fifteen yards.

That assignment ended shortly after that. In a way it was hard to let go of, cuz I gotta tell you, those armistice commission guys lived better in the field in Korea than I did years later traveling on a corporate expense account. Three hot meals a day, ice cream, fresh fruit and Cuban cigars—all free.

When we left the company to rotate home and arrived at ASCOM City, they formed us up into units for control purposes. Rock and I split up there. I saw him a couple of times aboard ship coming back to the USA, but upon arrival I was processed for immediate discharge and he was shipped off to another base. I'm sure he went back to Texas and resumed his business, which was being a florist.

I was not a big fan of draftees being put into "my Corps," but I would make an exception for the Rock. He could share my fighting hole anytime, anyplace.

Friends & Neighbors

After a breach in the MLR in October of 1952, at an area known to those who lived there as "The Hook," it was decided to shorten the amount of ground over which the 1st Marine Division was spread. The Hook had been the extreme eastern end of the terrain occupied by the Marines. As the Marine area of responsibility was shifted to the west, the positions vacated were occupied by troops from the Commonwealth. This division was comprised of Australians, Canadians, and troops from the United Kingdom itself. There seemed to be a mutual satisfaction in this arrangement. The Commonwealth units were glad to serve with the Marines on their flank and we considered the Brits, Aussies, and Canadians first class soldiers.

In all actuality I never did have contact with any of these troops on line. The closest we came to them on line was in February/March of '53 when the 5th Marines were on our division's right flank. However, between my outfit and the British was the 3rd battalion of the 5th. From where we were, we could tell when they were having a busy night by the flashes in the night sky and the rumble of gunfire large and small that reached our positions. The same was true for them and during the battle for Reno and Vegas the Commonwealth artillery played a large role in supporting the Marine efforts to reclaim the outposts.

There was one night in April when two other Marines and I got to meet some of these blokes up close and personal.

An old squad mate of mine who had been transferred to a motor transport outfit after recovering from a wound showed up at our reserve location one afternoon with a jeep. While we reminisced we drank all the beer we could beg, borrow, or buy, and we would have stolen some but there wasn't any. While bemoaning the situation someone mentioned that we should be Brits because they got a rum ration, blah, blah, blah. At the mention of this my friend with the jeep recalled that on his way from the rear he had passed a British reserve camp. In less time than it took to say "blimey" it was decided we would pay them a visit.

First, though, a few small problems had to be worked out. My friend had a pass for the jeep and himself that would get him through the sentries and checkpoints. My other friend and I didn't have one and we knew better than to ask for one. It was decided that just at dark our ex-squad member would drive out the main entrance from our bivouac and wait for me and my other friend just outside the sentries' fields of vision. We would cut across a couple of rice paddies and meet him there. What a plan!

It worked to perfection and we were off into the night. The ride was about a half hour until we pulled up at a sentry booth where there was a Black Watch private on duty. He asked our business and we told him we came to see if we could buy some beer or other spirits. He directed us to a large tent where he said we would find most of the troops and a lot of beer. We pulled up close to the tent, parked the jeep, and entered into what can only be described as a party in progress. Down one side of the tent were several trestle tables end-to-end that must have stretched twenty yards. The tables were covered with zinc tubs, each full of Asahi beer. Asahi is a Japanese beer and if I remember correctly is made from rice. What else in Japan? There were close to 100 British soldiers in the tent in various stages of inebriation and several small groups had formed to sing army songs. All the groups were not singing the same song or in the same place in the song but no one cared.

Once our presence became known we were the center

of attention and everyone's friend. Everyone wanted a keepsake. We lost all our Marine Corps emblems but did draw the line when some of our new found comrades suggested we trade weapons as souvenirs. We could not have been any more warmly welcomed and the evening was a huge success from my point of view. We still had the matter of getting back into our own area, but that could wait. We drank lots of Asahi and I learned the words to an old British military song that I still remember to this day. The words are as follows but you have to imagine the Brit accent that sounds more like Oy than I:

> I don't want to be a soldier
> I don't want to go to war
>
> I'd rather hang around
> Picadilly underground
>
> And live off the wages
> Of an highbrow lady
>
> I don't want a bayonet
> Up me arsehole
>
> I don't want me buttocks
> Shot away
>
> I'd rather stay in England
> Jolly, jolly England
>
> Rodgerin me bloody life away
> Gar Blimey
>
> Call out the Royal Territorials
> They'll keep England free
>
> Call out me mother, me sister or me brother
> But for Chrissake don't call me

Eventually a consensus was reached that we had better start back to our own camp and so with great gratitude we thanked our hosts and headed for the jeep—which would not start. It would not even try to start. Looking under the hood it didn't take long to see that the distributor cap was off and the rotor had been removed. Back into the tent, and after another couple of Asahis and a lot of begging, we got the parts we needed to get the engine started. Our friends weren't done yet. As we were saying our final farewells they loaded one of the zinc tubs full of beer into the back seat of the jeep.

As it turned out this was our salvation as far as getting back into camp. We hit a Marine MP checkpoint and it cost us six Asahi. We decided not to try to sneak in across the rice paddies because we might get shot or if caught be in deep shit. So we pulled right up to the camp entrance and the price of admission was six more Asahis. When we got back to our tent we had only three beers left in the tub. We sat on a stack of logs piled up close to the tent and had a nightcap. My friend had to leave and get the jeep back, which I guess he did because I never heard from him again. My other buddy and I hit the sack for what proved to be a very short night's sleep. I felt like hell the next day but it was worth it. Or as my friends of the evening before might say, "it was bloody well worth it!"

Showers

I don't know what unit was responsible for operating and maintaining the showers. Whoever it was, my helmet's off to them.

The shower units that I saw were all very similar. They consisted of two squad tents linked together end to end. They both had wooden floors made of widely spaced boards.

The first tent was where one disrobed on the way to the second tent. The clothes we took off were thrown into piles of trousers, jackets, socks, etc. I think that while the utility trousers and jackets were laundered and recycled, the socks and skivvies were burned. Wouldn't want to get a whiff of that smoke!

The second tent had an arrangement of pipes that ran parallel with the long axis of the tent. These pipes were about six feet above the wooden deck and at intervals of about three feet had showerheads that sprayed toward the center of the tent. My best guess would be that about twenty men could shower at a time. Outside the second tent was a large pumping machine that made a loud humming noise and somewhere in the maze of pipes was a capability to heat the water before spraying it on the grungy Marines. I am unsure what the source of the water may have been. Considering the volume of usage, I suspect they may have drilled a well.

It was necessary to impose limits on the amount of time men could stand under the shower. The hot water beating down on someone who has just come in from zero degree weather coupled with the fact he may have last showered thirty or more days ago tended to encourage languishing. The problem was with the group in tent #1, guys who had disrobed and discarded their clothes and were now standing around naked waiting to get into the hot shower tent. Even with two pot-bellied stoves glowing cherry red in tent #1 it was less than comfortable.

Upon exiting the shower it was necessary to return to the first tent. After drying off, each man joined a line to draw clean clothes where each was issued a clean utility jacket, trousers, skivvies, and a pair of socks. No attempt was made to accommodate anyone by size. You got clean stuff to wear and that was it. I once drew a utility jacket with master sergeant stripes stenciled on the sleeves that was large enough so that if I wanted to I think I could have worn it over my parka. No one cared about the fit or lack thereof. Just by being clean the clothes felt wonderful.

Shower points were usually a couple of miles behind the MLR. Depending on the position a unit occupied, a Marine might not get a shower until his unit was rotated to reserve. Even in reserve the weather might dictate the availability of showers.

My personal hygiene history as I recall was similar to this: While our unit was on hill 229, I was able to get to the rear for a shower in early December 1952. While in reserve in January 1953 our entire company was marched several miles to the nearest shower point. The weather was hovering in the zero range and when we arrived there were a couple of Marines working on or near the pump unit alongside the shower tent. What they were doing was running blow torches back and forth along the pipes leading from the pump to the shower tent. Our company executive officer checked inside and came back with the scoop. The shower would be operative in a few minutes—BUT—the water would not be heated! He asked if we wanted to go for it or come back tomorrow. How does someone who asks such a stupid question get to be an officer? The consensus was we would do like MacArthur and return. We did, and the next day everything was back in working order. We got clean and we got clean clothes. It was well we did, too. We returned to the lines in February and our next opportunity to shower was when we went into division reserve in April. Then in May the entire division rotated back to corps reserve and showers were accessible on at least a weekly basis. Better yet, we were given a second set of utilities and access to a Korean laundry service. From June, when the division went back into the line until the end of July when the ceasefire took effect it was back to the shower-a-month plan.

It sounds pretty bad but in fact we were all dirty and pretty much smelled the same. On line water came in five-gallon jerry cans that had to be carried up hill. This led to the establishment of very definite priorities for the use of water. First of course was drinking. Brushing teeth was second while washing and shaving was a distant third. It was not uncommon for all the guys in a bunker to wash their faces and shave from the same half helmet full of water, but not every day. Actually it may all have been part of a secret Marine Corp program titled "Shower Appreciation."

Dollar Bill

Dollar Bill

"Dollar Bill" was a nickname he brought with him from Chicago's South Side when he joined B-1-5 in April 1953. He was a tall, skinny black kid who tried to act hardboiled and had a line of jive a mile long.

Once he made up his mind about you, Dollar Bill either shut you out completely or presented an entirely different personality. It was remarkable to watch him go back and forth between personas as he interacted with different people.

One thing he went to great pains to keep a secret was the fact that he could neither read nor write at anywhere near a competent level. It was not uncommon to see him sitting on his cot with a newspaper or magazine pretending to be engrossed in the copy in order to keep his secret.

I learned of his literacy problem when he approached me privately and asked me to read him his mail. He later asked me if I would write a few letters for him. The fact that I kept this between the two of us must have impressed him because he became a dedicated friend.

After the ceasefire our outfit moved back to a former reserve area called Camp Rose. We had been there several months when Dollar Bill's number came up for mess duty. This is the equivalent of KP in the army, but in the Marines it is a 30-day assignment. Bill drew the assignment of being the battalion baker's assistant. The immediate benefit of this was that our squad now had instant access to fresh baked bread and the occasional tray of pastries.

At the end of his tour, Bill decided to extend on mess duty for another thirty days. At the time our company was digging positions at what was called the "Kansas Line," which would become our new defensive position should the ceasefire break down.

During his second tour in the bakery, the baker was called home on an emergency leave, and Dollar Bill was named the temporary replacement. The position included use of a jeep and trailer, which Bill would soon make good use of to the benefit of yours truly. A week or so later, it was learned that the baker would not be returning to Korea, and so Bill became the official baker of the 1st Battalion, 5th Marine Regiment.

My tour of duty in the "Land of the Morning Calm" was expiring. For a week or more prior to my rotation date, my tent mates and I had been hoarding our beer rations for a going home celebration, but the accumulation would not have lasted very long with the number of Marines who would be dropping in. Dollar Bill, to the rescue!

My friends began gathering in our tent early in the evening and there were probably close to forty troopers there. My platoon leader stopped in to donate a couple of bottles of hard liquor from the company officers and to wish me Godspeed. Just as he was leaving, Dollar Bill arrived and began organizing a work detail to unload the jeep and trailer that he had backed up to the tent. He had brought ten cases of beer and ten pizzas, which he had baked for the occasion.

Bill had done all of this unasked and at his own expense (although I suspect there was some bartering of mess hall stuff for the beer). He could only stay for a beer or two and had to get the jeep back. Before he left he said a few nice things to me, in private of course, and then he was gone, and I never saw him again.

It's strange how we became good friends and showed each other kindness and respect in a faraway land. Had we been home in Chicago, there would have been nothing to bring us together and innumerable barriers to keep us apart. I boarded a truck for ASCOM City around daybreak the next morning and left "B Co." 1st Battalion, 5th Marines. I also left behind some of the best friends and most cherished memories a man could ever hope to have.

*C Co. New Yorkers: Cy Worker (Brooklyn), Don
"Stumpy" Heller (New Rochelle), J.P. Heaphy
(Great Neck), and Armand "Blackie" Briere
(Lake George)*

Other Recollections and Ponderings

THE COLD: After the ordeal of the "Chosin Few" on their withdrawal to the sea, a guy would have to be a real wimp to bitch about the Korean winters. Well you're in the right place and have the right guy, Cpl. Wimp speaking. In the trench warfare in vogue in 1952-53, standing in a hole, wearing your entire wardrobe from dusk to dawn could be extremely chilling from November to March. During the day when we were in bunkers and allowed to use our sleeping bags, it wasn't so bad.

In reserve the situation was poor all the time. We were billeted in tents that were not as warm as bunkers. There were two pot-bellied stoves in each tent but the supply of oil would only support a few hours burn every evening. The remainder of the time the tents were unheated or we were outside in the elements anyway. While in reserve each man could get a three-can beer ration. This gift from on high was normally stored under one's cot. The foot of my cot was no more than 6 or 8 feet from one of the stoves and as often as not it was necessary to put the beer on the stove to return it to a liquid state for drinking. Occasionally the forming ice would push aside the pull tab and a finger of ice would rise through the hole like a skinny, beer popsicle.

The other thing that happened regularly and added to the feeling of being in an ice cave was the freezing of our breath as we exhaled. The mist caused by our breath would rise to the canvas of the ceiling and coat it with white frost.

Then during the night an icicle would form from the ceiling directly down to the breathing hole in each man's sleeping bag. Awakening to the white, frost coated ceiling and the stalactite-like icicles hanging down was indeed like waking in an ice cave. The mitigating factor here was that on most mornings we were rolled out of the sack before it was light enough to see just how cold it was.

In retrospect, I don't think any of us really suffered from the experience but we sure as hell learned a lot about discomfort.

RATS: I have never and have no immediate plans to spend any time at a major city landfill or touring a metropolitan sewer system. If I did, however, I would be hard-pressed to be made to believe that I would find a rat population larger than that of the Land of the Morning Calm. It is my considered opinion that the only things in Korea that outnumbered the Chinese were the rats.

On line they could be seen in the bunkers as they scuttled along the ceilings between the bottom row of sandbags and the supporting timbers. I recall one bunker where our makeshift bunks were arranged in an L shape. My buddy Joey and I slept on the lower tier with our feet at the intersection of the two legs of the L. At the top of the vertical leg of the L, where my head would be, was a kind of table we had made from ammo boxes. At some point during the first couple of days in that bunker I for some reason opened my eyes and looked up. I found my gaze being returned by six or eight beady little eyes less than a foot away. After that I slept with my feet closest to the table and relied on Joey's feet to deter visitors to the end where my head was.

In reserve it was the same, the rats were everywhere and in great numbers. Other than our packs we had no storage, so anything a person wanted to keep or store went under the cot. The rats quickly figured out that that was the place to be. We had two men bitten by rats in one reserve period and both were immediately evacuated to Japan. One trooper reached under his rack for something and was bitten on the wrist. The other poor devil was unaware that as he slept a rat had nestled under his chin to take advantage of the warmth of his breath. When the guy rolled over and startled the rat it bit him on the upper lip.

After a period of adjustment that went thru fear and revulsion and finally ended in hatred, we all learned to live with these little bastards—but never on friendly terms. Some guys, like my friend the Greek, would shoot at them inside the bunkers.

The memory that best recalls just how significant the rodent population was occurred one day just after we had come off line. We were establishing a new reserve camp on the reverse slope of a hill. I have long since forgotten the name given to this camp but I know it was named after a second lieutenant who was a KIA. The engineers had been there before we arrived and had terraced off the slope into shelves where we would be erecting squad tents.

Someone in the battalion decided that an attempt would be made to drive out the rats before we erected the tents. The companies were arranged in skirmish lines about 20 yards apart and facing uphill. Each man had an entrenching tool. The flamethrower guys from weapons company were sent up to the military crest facing downhill. On signal the flamethrowers began spraying the down slope while slowly advancing toward the deployed skirmish lines. What had a moment before appeared to be a lifeless hill suddenly became a writhing, squealing mass of motion. It was a bonafide rat stampede. There is no other way to describe this. We have all seen western movies where the cattle or buffalo herd runs off in a panic without a destination in mind, but intent on getting somewhere else. That's what we at the lower levels saw coming, but instead of cattle or buffalo, this was a stampede of rats.

As the tide flowed between and around our feet each man was bent at the waist and was swinging his entrenching tool as fast and as hard as he could. It was impossible to miss and every swing killed one or more of the herd.

Eventually the flamethrowers passed thru the last skirmish line and the surviving rats crossed a road and disappeared into the brush. The Korean Service Corps was put to work cleaning up the carcasses, which were dumped into a pit and burned again before being covered. We began unloading canvas and poles to erect the camp. The tents went up and we were moved in before dark; after dark the rats moved in.

SCARS: In today's world it seems I hear a great deal of yammering about how war and conflict leaves emotional scars on one's psyche. Maybe there's some validity somewhere in the psycho-babble that constitutes the discussions on this subject. Personally, I don't know squat about that stuff and I am either too old or too disinterested to learn. There may have been a few that I never rubbed shoulders with that have this affliction, but I never knew a single Marine in my generation who suffered from this post combat stress. Were we glad when the shooting stopped? Damn right! Were we sorry we shot back and maybe even hurt someone who was trying to kill us? Uh-uh! Not even a little bit!

When I think of scars it is the physical kind that come to mind. Of all the things that can happen to a guy in combat I think shrapnel wounds may be the worst. It seems that scars from shrapnel wounds have an angry quality about them that takes a long time to subside. It's almost as if the scar is angry that it is being forced to heal and to an observer it can have an appearance that is almost as painful to look upon as the original wound.

I base these comments on observations over time but in particular from one outing that took place in April 1953. We had moved into a rest area that had a shallow, wide, fast flowing stream running just behind our company tents. It was early April and we had a bright sunlit day. A large group of us wandered down to the creek to bathe. Our hands and faces were in stark contrast to the paleness of our bodies that hadn't been exposed to the sun or elements since the previous fall. We were an unhealthy, bleached out looking bunch for sure. What I observed was that the stark whiteness of the bodies made the scars on the guys who had been hit stand out like neon lights. It would be impossible to describe the variety of size and shapes in evidence of the wounds received. The common characteristic of all of them, even of those that were from wounds received months earlier, was that they seemed to resent having been treated and remained slightly swollen and an angry red color. I have to say though that the guys who bore these scars were too busy frolicking in the water and paid them a lot less heed than I did.

Sergeants

Gunnery Sergeants

Gunnery sergeants are commonly referred to as "Gunny" by both troops and officers. While the first sergeant of an outfit handles the administrative and paperwork details associated with running a Marine company, the gunny through the platoon sergeants runs the daily operations of the unit. That pretty much holds true whether it is a unit in training at a stateside base or one in a combat role overseas. In the history of the Corps there are many examples of Marines of this rank who have become legendary examples of dedication to duty and to their fellow Marines.

I was fortunate enough to serve with a few gunnies who were the perfect example of what a leader should be. When the hour was the darkest or the situation looked grim, the gunny would appear, jump into your hole and shoot the shit for a few minutes as though you were about to go on liberty and he was counseling you about not getting into trouble off base. There were others I knew who had an entirely different way of viewing the world or didn't exactly fit the mold.

I once overheard a conversation between a gunny and the company executive officer at Quantico that went something like this:

(The gunny was a married man and lived off base in the Washington D.C. area.)

X.O: Heading for home tonight Gunny?

Gunny: No Sir. I won't be going off base till my wife finds a new apartment.

X.O: Lease expire or are you having a problem with the apartment?

Gunny: Neither Sir. I have severed diplomatic relations with the District of Columbia.

X.O: What's that all about?

Gunny: Well Sir, the other night a motorcycle policeman pulled me over for speeding as I was on my way to the apartment. He told me that unless I had a good reason for speeding he would be giving me a ticket. I advised the young officer that I did indeed have just cause for speeding. I was on my way home to fornicate with the Mrs. Then that little son-of-a-bitch gave me a ticket. I went home and told my wife to find an apartment outside the D.C. metro area and that I would not be coming back into this place. I refuse to contribute to the economy of a town that penalizes a man for wanting to fornicate with his wife!

I don't know how all this ended up but it would only seem irrational to someone who wasn't acquainted with the gunny.

Another gunny story that has stayed with me over the years is one that is not in keeping with what one would expect of a gunnery sergeant, and that is probably why I remember it so well. The incident took place on one of our infamous wire laying details. It was January 1953, and we had been awakened back in the reserve area at about 2 a.m. and trucked forward to reinforce the wire obstacles in front of the MLR. The operation was being supervised by the gunnery sergeant of the unit occupying the trench positions in that segment of the line.

Work was proceeding as well as could be expected given the darkness and the brutally cold temperatures. As it came closer to daybreak we all began to look for the easiest and fastest way out of the wire and back to the trench. We had learned from previous wire laying details that as soon as it was light enough for us to be seen we became targets for the Chinese. This morning was no exception, and at the first scream of an incoming 76 round I was off to the relative safety of the trenches. The place where I rolled into the trench had what we called a "rabbit hole" dug into the forward wall of the trench. Rabbit holes were good places to crawl into in the event of airbursts and unless you were required to be up and shooting back, were cozy places to hide—sort of like a dirt womb.

By chance there was another Marine, nicknamed Rip, who had tumbled into the trench very near to me and we were both sitting with our backs to the rabbit hole wondering why there was no one else in the trench-line. It turns out that in our haste to find cover we had not reached the main trench but had jumped into a position inside of our wire but still forward of the MLR. This position was manned as a listening post at night—only at night because to get to or to leave this position in daylight was to expose oneself to the enemy's view. We more or less learned this through trial and error. Each time we would explore a route to the MLR we would draw fire and so we soon settled in to think things over. The wait was made less enjoyable by my companion's constant reminding me that the stuff the Chinese were throwing our way could not only severely maim a person but had the potential to kill you, too.

After about an hour of this shit I was ready to make a dash for it when we heard a noise coming from the trench to our left. We were both ready to shoot if necessary when around the bend on his hands and knees comes the gunny. Hooray! We are saved! Here's the gunny, yippee! He crawls up to our rabbit hole, looks us in the eye and asks "Whadda ya think we oughta do?" I cannot tell you how disappointed I was at that moment. Gunnies aren't supposed to ask PFCs what they think—they're supposed to tell us what to do.

I told them that I was going down the trench as far to the right as I could and then I was going to make a run up the hill for the main trench. They could follow and we could all break at the same time or they could stay here. I was going. I crawled away and they stayed there. When I got to the end of the position trench I leaped out and ran uphill as fast as I could. I was not shot at and made it OK. Over the next half hour the other two also made it safely back to the trench. The gunny stayed on the line with his unit and Rip and I boarded trucks behind the reverse slope and were taken back to the reserve area. I was glad to get back to the area where I felt like we had a much better gunnery sergeant looking out for our interests than the guys we had left behind on line did.

First Sergeants

The experiences I had with first sergeants varied greatly between my first and second enlistments. During the initial three years I would have to say my interactions with these icons of the Corps were mostly unpleasant. When it wasn't being unpleasant, I think antagonistic would be a good adjective to describe our relationship. In fairness to these unit administrators, I was something of a pain in the ass from time to time.

While I was in the 6th Marines I made the first sergeant's shit list but I was not near the top. I irritated him severely by writing a letter to Headquarters Marine Corps outside of the chain of command, and later came back a couple of days late from a leave period. He never showed any evidence that he had taken any of these incidents personally. While I never made the list for promotion to corporal, I never attributed that to the first sergeant.

Later in this first hitch I transferred overseas and shortly after I arrived there the company got a new first sergeant. He and I did not get off to a very good start. A few days after his arrival I blew up a four-hole crapper by pouring too much gasoline in it before burning the contents. Shortly after that episode we went back on line and I had little or no contact with him for about forty-five days. In retrospect all the problems between the first sergeant and I occurred when we were in reserve areas.

The next time we went into reserve the deck was kind of stacked against me. The tent I was assigned to and was also the senior man in was the closest tent to the quonset hut that served as the company office and the first sergeant's quarters. Within a day or two after moving into this area another episode occurred. One of the guys in my squad, a skinny little runt called J.J. from Scully Square in Boston, had a little too much to drink and ended up in a fight with a guy from the 3rd platoon. Actually it couldn't have been much of a fight because by the time I was notified and arrived on the scene, it was over and J.J. was a lot worse for wear.

Wanting to know why this all happened, I mosied down to the 3rd platoon area and asked the other party in the scuffle what had brought it on and why he couldn't have given J.J. a pass since clearly he was in no condition to defend himself. It soon became obvious to me that this guy was flushed with victory and had delusions of invincibility. We were both PFCs, but while he was still a rifleman I was an acting squad leader and was not about to take any crap from this guy. His squad leader, a buck sergeant and a friend of mine, unsuccessfully tried to put a lid on the situation. We ended up in the company street just outside of his tent.

There was a crowd of spectators that had gathered and

I was a little uneasy because most of them were from the 3rd platoon. Once we started fighting I wondered how this guy had even been able to whip J.J. I knocked him down several times and each time allowed him to get back up. After another knockdown he gathered himself on his hands and knees and instead of rising, lunged and tackled me. We rolled around for a minute or two and I was able to end up straddling his chest in such a way that both his arms were pinned to his sides. I was about to offer him the opportunity to surrender, but to be sure he would recognize the consequences of not doing, I raised my right fist as a threat that he would see.

Just at that moment someone behind me grabbed the collar of my jacket and tried to pull me over backwards. Of course my first thought was that it was one of his squad mates, so I resisted and reacted. I pulled loose, rolled off to one side, and came back to my feet ready to assault whoever it was that had grabbed me. There stood the first sergeant. I think maybe he wished I would have slugged him (and I almost did) so he could have had a go at whipping my ass, or at least he could have sent me to the brig for striking someone of higher rank. Once the fight was stopped and he had disbursed the crowd, he never mentioned it to me again. However, every month the platoon commanders were directed by the captain to send one man from their unit to him for an interview and possible meritorious promotion. I was sent several times and dismissed by the first sergeant before the captain even knew that I had been sent. Eventually I made corporal through normal channels in spite of him. It did bother me that while he held things I might have done against me he never gave me any credit for the things I had done right. Don't ask me for an example but there must have been a few.

The next incident with this six striper happened maybe two weeks after the fight described above. The enemy had no air force to speak of in our area of operations. There was, however, a single airplane that on occasion would fly over reserve areas at night. I have no knowledge of that aircraft ever causing a casualty on our side. In fact, he was considered a source of humor among the troops. The nickname given him, based on the sound of his engine, was "Washing Machine Charlie."

I mentioned earlier that the tent that I habitated was the one in closest proximity to the first sergeant's quarters. On one particular evening several things transpired simultaneously that gave the old fart another reason to jump my ass. I had crawled in the sleeping bag early this particular night. There was a poker game in progress in the tent at the time Washing Machine Charlie decided to pass over the area. I remained asleep, oblivious to the poker game and the air raid warning that sounded to announce Charlie's passage. The first sergeant, on the other hand, took it seriously enough to take a walk through the company area and ensure that black out procedures were in effect. They were. That is, everywhere except our tent. Here the poker players had not closed the vent in the roof and a column of lantern light was being projected into the night sky. He had them close the flap and left instructions for the senior man in the tent to report to him in the morning.

I suspected I was in some kind of trouble when I was advised of the instruction. I went to the office in the morning and promptly made things worse by telling the clerk "the first sergeant wants to see me." He overheard this and came roaring out to advise me that his instructions had been to have me report to him, and he had said nothing about wanting to see me. Having clarified that, he then told me to report in a manner that Marines are taught, one that reflects respect for the person being reported to. I think I surprised him because I knew how to do this and did so in a military manner. His next order was for me to go to the supply shed and come back with a shovel, a rake, and a wheelbarrow. When I got back to the quonset hut he took me outside and showed me a large open area adjacent to the company office. It was approximately 100 to 125 yards long and about equally wide. He advised me that I had been relieved of all other duties until such time as this area had been turned into a parade field. He had made arrangement to have sand trucked in and I was to spread it and rake it until he agreed that it was indeed a parade field. It took me a week or so and it wasn't so bad. As long as I looked busy he never bothered me and no one else would interfere with the first sergeant's personal labor force. Eventually our unit rotated back into the front lines and again I completely lost contact with my favorite sergeant.

In July of 1953 there was an accord reached that both sides would stop shooting, dismantle their fortifications, reduce their frontline forces and move back a specified distance from the positions held at the agreement. Two of the three regiments in our division moved south of the Imjin River, and my regiment stayed north of the river. The purpose of our presence was to act as an early warning system in the case of a truce violation. The whole thing was a set-up for the first sergeant to once again find unpleasant things for me to do. In the territory that today is known as the "DMZ" it was our regiment's duty to man roadblocks during the hours of darkness all along the sector. This was really crappy duty. It would be two marines with side arms and a radio, trucked out to these positions just as day was ending, and we were there for the night until picked up after dawn the next day. I think there was a perverse sense of revenge or something in the first sergeant's mind because on occasion he would tell my partner and I not to go on the truck—he and the driver would take us out in the company jeep and post us on watch. I think he liked the idea of leaving us there with no shelter of any sort and returning to the relative comfort of the company area.

I managed to piss him off a couple of more times without even trying. During the time we were manning these roadblocks I received two phone calls on the first sergeant's phone. One was a friend of mine in the 7th Marines who had been assigned to Freedom Village for the prisoner exchanges and wanted to know if I would care to be assigned there also. The other call came from a friend from the old neighborhood in Chicago. This friend was in the Air Force in Japan, serving in a communications unit. He knew what my organization was and on a flyer put through a call. We were both surprised it got thru and the top felt it necessary to remind me that this was not a public phone.

I guess if there was any satisfaction at all in the relationship it was twofold. First was the fact that when I left, the Korean winter was about to kick into high gear and he was still gonna be there. Secondly, I got away with telling him how I felt about things before I left. The night before I left camp for rotation home there was a rather wild party in our tent. Fortunately, this time the tent was far-removed from the company office. The party lasted well into the wee hours of the morning. I was supposed to board a truck down by the road around 6 a.m. I knew that if I crapped out chances were slim that I would wake by 6, so I carried my gear down to the road and planned to sit there for the few remaining hours. Everyone had passed out or gone to sleep and I was still in possession of the better part of a fifth of whiskey that had been donated by one of the officers in the company.

The scheduled pick-up point was at the bottom of the hill below the company office. I dragged my gear down there and sat on my sea bag, not a bit tired and surprisingly not too cold considering this was November. I had a little time to kill so I decided to go say so long to the gunny. The company office was a squad tent divided in two parts. The front was the office. A rope strung across the tent was hung with several blankets behind which were the quarters of the two ranking enlisted men in the company, the gunny and my nemesis the first sergeant. There were no locks on the tents so I sauntered right into their sleeping quarters. Once I identified who was who, I sat on the edge of the gunny's cot and gently nudged him on the forehead with the whiskey bottle. He sat up and asked what was wrong. I said, "Nothing's wrong. I'm leaving and I would like you to have a drink with me. That brought him to a sitting position and he said he would be glad to have a farewell drink with me. At some point in here the first sergeant rolled over and said, "Is that you Easton?" I said, "Yep." He asked if I was going to offer him a drink. I told him, "You might as well go back to sleep, you Irish prick. I'd pour this out before I would share it with you!" His comment was, "You had better not miss that truck in the morning." I knew he was right and so I said my farewells to the gunny and meandered back down the hill. I was glad to see the truck come before the first sergeant got up in the morning.

During my second enlistment I had much better relations with the first sergeants in all the units I served in, not because they were that much different but because I had become a much better Marine. I have never been certain but there was also always a feeling I had that once you signed for a second go around, these Old Salts thought you were more worth their attention than someone who was just passing through their Corps.

One incident worth mentioning did occur when I was serving in the 2nd Recon Battalion. My wife and I were living off post in Wilmington, North Carolina. She was pregnant and her delivery date looked like it was going to happen over the Labor Day weekend. The good ol' boy country doctor that was caring for her had a fishing trip planned for that weekend so he decided and she agreed that labor would be induced. All the arrangements were made and I went in to see the first sergeant and requested a 96-hour pass. He asked me why I needed the pass. I told him my wife was having a baby on September 1st and I would be bringing her and the child home from the hospital. At that pronouncement he pushed his chair back and asked me, "What are you, some kind of fucking prophet?" I explained to him about the induced labor arrangement. He then told me if I came back to camp I better have a birth certificate. If I didn't come back, someone better send or bring him a death certificate. Those were the only two conditions under which he would grant the pass. I agreed to both, got the pass, and all went well.

Sergeant Majors

To me, sergeant major is the most awesome rank in the Marine Corps. Other than a chest full of ribbons, there aren't too many things as militarily impressive as a Marine sergeant major's sleeve when he is in either dress blues or greens. The three chevrons with the four rockers and a star in the center sitting above anywhere from 5 to 7 or 8 hashmarks, each representing four years of service, is truly a sight to behold. In most cases the individual whose sleeve is described here will also be wearing a chest full of medals or ribbons.

In all honesty my contact with these exalted creatures was rather limited. That's not all bad. On my first enlistment, the only contact I had with a sergeant major was when he marched me into the colonel's office so I could enlighten him on the facts of my latest transgression against God, country and Corps.

On my second enlistment the sergeant major of the battalion I was in had previously been the first sergeant of the company I was assigned to. Surprise! Surprise! When he was the first sergeant of the company he and I had a very good relationship. He frequently singled me out for special assignments and I was fortunate enough to fulfill his expectations. One of these details was being designated as the company chaser. The duties of this position were to move Marines who were coming from or going to the brig as directed. They might be going to sick call for a pre-incarceration physical or to battalion headquarters for court martial proceedings.

It was during one such activity that I was given the opportunity to go on embassy duty. I had picked up a prisoner at the post brig and taken him to HQ where there was a court martial in progress. His attorney, who was a commissioned officer, took the prisoner into a room for private consultation and I was standing at the door in the hallway. The sergeant major came down the hall with a sheaf of papers in his hand. When he arrived opposite me he asked, "Would you like to go on embassy duty?" I said, "Absolutely!" He told me to return to the area after I had delivered the prisoner back to the brig and he would send word to the company first sergeant. I did as I was instructed, but upon my return to the company, when I stopped in at the company office and inquired about the timing of the move it caused quite a stir. The company had not yet been notified, and the first sergeant was more than a little annoyed that I would be telling him what my plans were instead of vice-versa. I referred him to the battalion sergeant major and beat a hasty retreat. The orders came through later that day and I was on my way in less than a week to Marine Security Guard School.

Marine Security Guard School, oh yes. This is where I met the next and last sergeant major with whom I had contact. The sergeant major of whom I write was unquestionably the meanest bastard I ever met in the service. It was his job to shake out the candidates for embassy duty who in his judgment lacked the proper degree of motivation or whose assignment to a diplomatic post might result in an international incident. He did a respectable job in my estimation as we only graduated about a third of the candidates. I should mention that the sergeant major's assignment prior to taking over the administration of the school was as brig warden at a naval prison.

His bag of tricks was divided about equally between those intended to cause mental stress and others that put a physical strain as the focus of his attention. In many ways it was similar to boot camp in that there seemed to be no let up to the harassment or the level of intensity. This was hard to take the first week or so because we were no longer boots, and in almost every case the candidates were non-commissioned officers. After the first week I found it entertaining as long as I wasn't the one in the box. However, the fact that I could smile, or in some cases even laugh, about things had to be a well-kept secret, otherwise I could find myself receiving double of whatever prompted the smile.

Just a few of the Sgt. Major's remedies for lapses in military efficiency or what he perceived to be out of line:

Hands in Pockets: Sent to Special Services to check out a pair of boxing gloves that the guilty party then was required to wear from reveille to taps for the remainder of the school term.

Falling out for Physical Drill at 5:30 a.m. without a belt: When it was determined that the missing belt was in the candidate's locker box, the solution was simple. For the remainder of the term this candidate would carry his locker box to all formations when he was not under arms. This included classes and chow.

An accidental discharge of a blank cartridge during a ceremonial firing drill: It was decided that this student could not be trusted with a real rifle. He was sent to the post carpenter shop to requisition a 42-inch piece of 2 x 4. When he returned with the lumber the Sgt. Major provided him with a pen knife and instructed him to carve a rifle with which he could be trusted. When this rifle was complete he would be designated as the class chaser.

A red necktie found in one of the wall lockers during locker inspections: The immediate concern was how this would look with the Marine's uniform. He was sent to the head to change neckties (called field scarves). Upon his return the sergeant major announced that he thought it looked OK but only a communist would wear a red field scarf and so he was convinced that this student was a subversive. The Marine so accused and deemed guilty was instructed that effective immediately he would no longer be part of the unit. As we marched from place to place he was to position himself six paces to the rear and as his left foot struck the ground he was to sound off, "I'm a Communist!" The sergeant major then called for the rifle carver and told him we have a communist in our midst and you are responsible to watch him. The guy with the wooden rifle was to march six paces behind the communist with his 2 x 4 rifle at port arms and each time the communist sang out "I'm a Communist," the rifle bearer as his right foot hit the ground was to sound off "I'm keeping an eye on him!"

I could go on about the mind games for a couple of more pages but I think a reader gets the idea that the man was a master at what he was trying to accomplish. If he could make you angry enough to quit or become antagonistic there was no way he was going to allow you to finish the course and later blow up with a foreign national. His favorite warning was that while you might finish the course he could still see to it that you ended up serving in Kabul or Ougadougou. Somehow over the years, and I'm sure it's not just me, when I look back on these episodes I can't help but think of the sergeant major with respect and admiration.

Red

It is surprising, even to me, that if I were asked to classify all the people I have known over the years, Red would be one of the top five most unforgettable characters I ever met. This is even more surprising when it is considered that our association was only for a little over a year.

What makes Red so unforgettable was his sheer delight in being alive and his ability to infect those around him with the same feelings. Things were never too tough for Red, and if you were down he always had a way of picking you up. That's not to say that being a friend of Red's was always easy. There was an unspoken obligation to being his friend. He just assumed that the bond between his friends and himself meant that they would go as far for him as he was prepared to go for them, which was all the way.

It was pure coincidence that brought us together in early 1957. We were both Korean Conflict veterans who, after trying civilian life for a few years, had reenlisted in the Marine Corps. We both reported to Quantico on the same day and were assigned adjacent bunks in Casual Company.

For the uninitiated, a casual company is the military equivalent of a holding pen. People assigned here are in transit of some sort, perhaps awaiting discharge or transfer or for medical reasons, while their orders and the typical reams of paperwork in all things government sponsored were processed. In our case, we were awaiting assignments and being issued new uniforms. Also in this mix were two slick-sleeve privates who had just been released from the brig and who were awaiting bad conduct discharges. A major problem with casual companies is that because everyone is in transit, there is no permanent cadre of NCOs and there is a resultant lack of discipline.

Which leads into how Red and I became acquainted. For each of the first couple of nights in the barracks, the aforementioned privates came in after lights out, very drunk, very loud, and obviously looking for trouble. Left unchallenged they would soon either go to sleep or pass out. On the third or fourth night they again came in late and decided to terrorize a young kid in the bottom rack across the aisle from me. This youngster was 17 or 18 years old and was awaiting an administrative discharge because he was unable to cope with the stress of training. Anyway, one of these clowns straddled the kid, pinning his arms under the blanket and began slapping his face. The other one hovered next to the bunk making threatening remarks. When it became apparent that there was to be no other intervention, I said, "Leave that kid alone and hit the sack!"

The immediate reaction from these two would-be bad asses was to leap into the aisle and demand to know who had said that. As if we had been rehearsing the move, Red and I both jumped out of our top bunks and said in unison, "I did." These two morons looked us over and, after getting a good look at Red, decided life out of the Corps would be better with teeth and quietly retired. That was the last time they acted up in the squad bay prior to their release from service.

To get an idea of what Red was like physically, I would suggest that you conjure up a mental image of a guard on a small college football team, but one with a linebacker mentality like Jack Lambert or Dick Butkus. He was just a shade under six feet tall, with red hair (of course) that he kept in a brush cut. His shoulders were very broad and he basically had no neck. There was usually a smile on his face and he reminded me of a large leprechaun. The best way I can think of to describe Red angry would be to ask you to visualize a young Mike Tyson in the first round of a championship fight.

Eventually we received assignments that would keep both of us at Quantico. Because of my infantry MOS, I was sent to an outfit called "Schools Demonstration Troops," SDT for short. Red had a tanker MOS and was sent to the post-armored unit. The SDT barracks was located mainside, within walking distance of just about everything, including the Enlisted Men's Club, more familiarly known as the "Slopchute." The armor park on the other hand was out in the boondocks and so I assumed this would mean that I would see Red only occasionally. Not so!

I mentioned earlier that Red had a zest for life and over the next year I was to learn just how much energy he devoted to enjoying himself. I also mentioned earlier that it wasn't always easy being his friend. I in no way meant that he was hard to like, but he was extremely hard to keep up with and he didn't give a person much choice. Due to the geography of the base he had to pass my barracks to get anywhere and so it became his custom to stop in and insist that I go with him, wherever he happened to be bound for. He would have made a great salesman because he never accepted no for an answer. Eventually I quit resisting because the evenings were usually a lot of fun.

Before I go any further and give an impression that Red was just a good-time Charlie, let me tell you what kind of Marine he was. During a combined infantry/tank operation in Korea, the enemy counterattacked in overwhelming numbers, forcing the infantry to fall back. This left the tanks isolated in the midst of the swarms of gooks. The tankers were spraying each other's vehicles with machine gun fire to keep the goonies off. It was while all of this was going on that Red was advised by radio that his tank was on fire over the engine compartment. He opened the hatch, climbed out, grabbed a shovel and, with gooks all around, threw dirt on the flames and extinguished the blaze before the engine was damaged. His tank and crew were able to return to the safety of the Marine lines. He was decorated for this action, but unless you saw him in dress uniform, you would never have been aware of this fact, and certainly would never have heard it from him.

He and I would frequently attend the "Rat Race,", which was the name Marines had bestowed on the Saturday night dance at the EM Club. The government would bring in several busloads of young ladies from the D.C. area, mostly clerks and secretaries in government offices. It was typical of Red to ask a young lady to dance and then come alongside and say, "Dave, I'd like you to meet my new mistress."

The Marine Corps, and I'm sure the other branches of service as well, have a lot of tough characters in their ranks. There are probably an even greater number in each service who believe themselves to be tougher than they are. Red was definitely one of the former and while very hard to provoke would never back away when reason failed. After a few scuffles of short duration with Red being the easy winner, he acquired a reputation on post of someone to be left alone. That is except for some of the tough guy personalities who had trouble accepting that there might be someone on post considered tougher than they fancied themselves. In many ways it was reminiscent of the gunfighter stories from the Old West. These "bad" guys would have a few beers and seek Red out in hopes of being able to tell everyone that "Red wasn't so hard to whip." To the best of my knowledge no one was ever able to honestly make that statement.

One particular evening in Quantico stands out in my memory. Red showed up at my barracks and said, "get dressed and we'll go to Fredericksburg." I declined, telling him I only had two bucks to my name. No sweat says he, he had it covered. I knew resistance would only delay our departure and so off we went to the pick-up station on Route 1, just outside the main gate. We had no trouble getting a ride and in short order were sitting in a roadside tavern in Fredericksburg. There was a bowling machine in the tavern. The pins were suspended and a heavy metal disk was used to simulate the bowling ball. The machine would accommodate four players and it cost ten cents per player to operate the machine.

We ordered two beers and I put my two bucks on the bar. Red added his bankroll to my two and before the beers were paid for we had between us nine bucks and change. My first thought was that it had been a long way to come for the two or three beers we could afford. Before I could pose this question to Red he had noticed three guys playing the bowling machine and went over to speak with them. He came back after a minute, took a dime from our collective wealth and became the fourth player. After a couple of frames had been bowled and he was waiting his turn to bowl, he came to the bar for a sip of his beer. That's when he told me the three losers each had to pay the winner ten bucks. He returned to the game and I being the saner of the two began a search for the closest exit. Not too much later Red returned, threw thirty dollars on the bar, ordered us two more beers, and returned to the game.

We not only got out of there alive, but after drinking our fill of beer, and of course magnanimous Red even bought a couple for the losers, Red still had more than seventy dollars in his pocket. On our way back to camp we stopped at the Iwo Jima Café, and Red bought us a steak and egg breakfast. I repeat myself, I know, but being a friend of Red's wasn't always easy. But then, it was rarely dull either.

One day early in 1958, Red told me he had received orders transferring him to Okinawa. He had leave on the books and was authorized to take delay in route but had no desire to visit his home before going overseas. I also had accrued leave coming and hadn't been home in a little over a year, so we decided I would take leave and Red and I would spend a week at my parent's house in Chicago. Red had a prepaid ticket to California and a large travel advance so we decided to go by train.

We left from Union Station in D.C. on an overnight train for Chicago. We were not very far from the station when Red made two discoveries. The first was the proximity of the club car from our seats. The second was that among our traveling companions on the train there was a large group of Naval personnel who had just completed boot camp. In this case the boot camp had been in Bainbridge, Maryland, and the brand new sailors were all women. Wanting to be sure these young ladies all got off to a good start in their military careers, Red herded them into the club car and with the help of his advance travel allowance made sure a good time was had by all. Early the next morning as we were passing thru western Indiana, Red notified me that he had extended the hospitality of my parents home to several of the WAVES, and we were to rendezvous with them at the station in downtown Chicago. My response to Red was to get his gear together and I told him we would be detraining at 79th Street and not the Loop station. He did, we did, and I have no idea what the young ladies did.

My best friend in Chicago was an Irishman named Sullivan. He and Red, who was also of Irish descent, hit it off immediately. Sully, when he could not be with us, allowed us the use of his car so that we had transport. Naturally I took Red around to all my old haunts and introduced him to the bartenders and friends who were in the various places. He got along famously with everyone, as I knew he would, and years later I would occasionally see someone that had met him and they would ask, "Whatever happened to your red-headed buddy?"

It so happened that our stay in Chicago encompassed St. Patrick's Day. This is a big deal in Chicago, particularly in neighborhoods where there is a large Irish contingent. The Chicago River is dyed green for the day, the center stripe on West 79th Street is painted green, and the specialty of the day in every bar is beer that has also been dyed green. I being of English heritage would not normally frequent Irish pubs and particularly not on St. Pattie's Day. Neither Sully nor Red would even consider not celebrating the occasion Irish style and so away we went to 79th Street. We began visiting the pubs well before noon, and by the time the parade started at 1 p.m. they both had green lips, tongues, and teeth. I suppose I was in the same condition but I couldn't see me. Both of these guys were highly personable and in mingling with the crowds, it wasn't long before we were all invited to several private parties. These parties were being held in halls with names like "Sons of Shannon."

What I discovered at the first club we visited was that we were obliged to sign a guest book to obtain entry. Their names being Sullivan and Flynn they easily passed the scrutiny of the doorkeepers. No way was I gonna let these watchdogs know a bloomin' Englishman was trying to crash their party. I quickly recalled a guy's name who had attended grammar school with me and signed his name, Frances Houlihan. Fortunately, there was not an accompanying ID check. The fact that Red and I were both in uniform also helped not only our access but the good citizens of 79th Street were most generous in seeing that we had full glasses and plenty to eat. It was nice to see the friendship between Sully and Red develop and hilarious to me to watch the two of them participating in the native Irish dancing. This excursion lasted well into the next morning and remains as fresh in my mind today as though it was yesterday.

Another incident which occurred during our Chicago trip was the night I lost Red. We had been out visiting some of the neighborhood high spots. At one of these places someone asked me for a ride home. I told Red where I was going and that I would be back for him shortly. When I returned he was gone. Everyone I asked knew exactly who I was looking for but no one knew where he had gone.

I started revisiting all the places we had been the last couple of nights. In several of the places the answer was, yes, he had been there, but again no one knew where he had gone. Having called in all the places I could think of and with the time getting close to 2:30 a.m., I decided Red could take care of himself and just maybe he had decided to go to my parent's house, so I headed for home. When I arrived at home, Red was not there. I was taking off my shoes when my mother came into the room and asked where my friend was. When I told her I had no idea, she said, "Well, you can't leave him out on the streets. Go find him!"

So, on with the shoes and back out into the night in search of Red I go. Due to the time, my list of places was now shortened to only the after-hour joints. Of course, knowing Red, one of my concerns was that he had discovered places I was not even aware existed. No one remembered seeing him recently but said if he came in they would see that he got to my folk's place. Having run out the string of places to look, I once again headed home, all the while trying to figure out how I was going to placate my mother and get some sleep.

I parked Sully's car and had started up the front steps when a voice behind me said, "Boy, am I glad to see you!" It was Red emerging from the back seat of my brother in-law's Buick, which was also parked at the curb. He explained that he had been sleeping there for a couple of hours before he heard me slam the car door. He had not wanted to go into the house without me because he was afraid my mother might make him go out and look for me.

As the day approached when Red would have to leave for California, he mentioned that his travel advance money had pretty much evaporated. A lot of it was spent the first night, on the train to Chicago. My brother-in-law, who was also a Korean War vet, floated me a loan and between Sully and I we got Red headed in the direction of Okinawa on time.

My friend Sully may have been glad to see us leave. He got his car back not much the worse for wear. Bob was a good catholic Irish boy and attended mass every Sunday. He told me later that for several Sundays after Red and I had left he would take his prayer book from the glove compartment of his car and go into church. There, during the service when he would turn to the appropriate page a small hand written note from Red would drop out, most of them not in keeping with the reasons Sully was in church.

When I returned to Quantico, life was less exciting and it took me awhile to get over expecting Red to barge into the squad bay with a plan for the evening. A few months later I was transferred to embassy duty in Brussells, and after that to Camp LeJeune to finish out my enlistment. During my assignment at LeJeune, I would run across Marines who had recently returned from Okinawa, and always asked them if they knew Red. Not many could say they actually knew him, but almost to a man they knew of him.

With only two or three days left in the Corps, I was sent to the post disbursing office to square away my final pay. As I exited the building I ran smack into Red. He had just returned from overseas and was being assigned to the tank battalion at LeJeune. He was reenlisting for six more years and had business in the disbursing office. Since our last meeting we had both become Buck Sergeants, and so we agreed to meet at the NCO Club that evening. Except for the missing tip of one ear which he had lost in a brawl, he looked exactly as I remembered him.

When Red showed up that evening at the NCO Club it was with a master plan on how we should spend the remainder of my enlistment celebrating our reunion. He also had a long list of reasons why I should reconsider and sign on for six more years in the Corps. With 48 hours left to do and a wife and child waiting for me in Chicago, I was able to resist all of his logic and enthusiasm. We remained on the post and drank a fair number of beers paid for with his reenlistment bonus. We laughed rehashing old times and parted company knowing we would always be friends.

I'm sorry, and a bit ashamed, to say I have no idea where Red is today but I am sure that if he could have his way he would spend his days in the turret of a tank and his evenings at the slopchute with his friends. I am very proud and consider myself very fortunate to have been his friend even if for all too brief a period. Semper Fi, Red.

Afterword

The fact that I am writing an afterword won't mean much to anyone else, but to me it signifies a final step in the conclusion of this project. The incidents and people I have written about here are finally, once again, seeing the light of day after existing only inside my head for the past fifty-some years.

All of what is written is about people who really lived and incidents that really happened. In telling of the various tales I have on occasion portrayed events in a lighter vein than prevailed while they were occurring. I did so in hopes of making the collection more reader friendly.

It has been more than fifty years since I have been in the Marine Corps, but there has not been a day pass in that span when I did not consider myself a Marine. As the old sayings go: "Once a Marine always a Marine" and the other is "You are a Marine till you die. Then you are a dead Marine." The pride I take in having served as a Marine does not come from any sense of personal accomplishment; it is derived from being able to state that the men I have written about and many more like them accepted me as a friend and fellow Marine.

Anyone who has been in combat will tell you that when the shit is really hitting the fan, things like patriotism, the flag, and even the folks at home become very remote. You and your squad mates are fighting for yourselves and for each other. In the Marines, in some crazy convoluted way, you are, without even being aware of it, also fighting to preserve the traditions established by Marines who preceded you in battles fought long ago. I have not explained this phenomenon very well but Marines will understand.

There have been significant changes in the Corps since I last stood formation. The uniforms, equipment, weaponry, and firepower have all been improved. Perhaps the most beneficial improvements have been those made in communications, allowing troops at all levels of command to better understand and react to an ever-changing scenario on a battlefield or in close combat. Today's training also puts more emphasis on physical conditioning, which is a good thing. However, I believe that the one constant in all of this time lapse is the individual who enlists to become a Marine and responds to the drill instructors and later to his non-commissioned officers to become a first class fighting man by anyone's measure.

To all Marines—past, present, and future—God bless you and Semper Fidelis.

About the Author

Dave Easton was born on Chicago's South Side in 1932. He joined the Marines at age 18 and served from January 1951 until January 1954, with the time after boot camp split between the 2nd Division in North Carolina and the 1st Division in Korea. After being honorably discharged he succeeded in acquiring an apprenticeship with the world's largest commercial printer, but recognizing a need for a more disciplined lifestyle, Dave re-enlisted in the Marines for another three-year hitch in February 1957. A couple of years into this enlistment he agreed to a two-year extension to qualify for embassy duty. Following training in Washington, D.C., he reported to the U.S. Embassy in Brussels, Belgium. While there Dave met and married Barbara. Dave finished his enlistment in C Company, 2nd Recon Battalion and was again honorably discharged in February 1962, and he resumed his interrupted apprenticeship. A couple of years later an opportunity came along to serve overseas with the Foreign Service of the Department of State, and the whole family spent the next couple of years in Rabat, Morocco. In 1966, he resigned from government employ and returned to his previous employer yet again. Over the course of the next twenty-four years he and the family (two daughters and a son) would move to locations in Indiana, Connecticut, and Tennessee. When the nest emptied, Dave and Barbara moved to Warsaw, Indiana, where they currently enjoy a relatively peaceful retirement.